Woodcarving

WOODCARVING
A MANUAL OF TECHNIQUES
Reg Parsons

The Crowood Press

First published in 1989 by
The Crowood Press Ltd
Ramsbury, Marlborough
Wiltshire SN8 2HR

Paperback edition 1993

This impression 1994

British Library Cataloguing-in-Publishing Data

Parsons, Reg
  Woodcarving: a manual of techniques.
  1. Woodcarvings. Techniques
  I. Title
  731.4'62

  ISBN 1 85223 770 8

Acknowledgements

Ashley Iles Tool Manufacturers, and Mr Keith Sawmy, who
commissioned the bookend carving of Hector.

Line illustrations by Andrew Mackintosh.

Printed and bound in Great Britain by
BPC Hazell Books Ltd
A member of
The British Printing Company Ltd

Contents

Introduction

Those who work with wood, whether they are cabinet makers, carpenters, or woodcarvers, start with a built-in advantage over all other artist craftsmen, for the material in which they work possesses a deep and lasting beauty that cannot be found in any other medium. It has its drawbacks, of course, but treated with love, respect and understanding, the only limit to what can be carved from wood is the carver's imagination. It is all there, just waiting to be uncovered.

The superb skills of Grinling Gibbons and medieval carvers took many years to acquire, but it will be found that adequate dexterity with carving tools can be gained quite quickly, even for those who have never handled a cutting tool of any description before. This leaves the carver to make full imaginative use of all the wonderful qualities of wood, its strength, colour, warmth, grain, scent, tactility, and permanence. It is as well to remember from the outset that today's carvings could well last for centuries and will be seen by, and give pleasure to, a great many people, in many cases being handed down in a family as heirlooms.

Although today the professional carver can spend many hundreds of pounds on tools and equipment it is quite possible for the beginner to make a start with very little outlay. Indeed most of the remarkable and beautiful work that has survived the centuries was carved with a handful of home-made tools, most almost certainly fashioned by the village blacksmith. In fact the simplest form of carving, whittling, only requires the use of a sharp knife. The purchase, however, of three or four suitable gouges will considerably widen the carver's scope and form the basis for a kit of tools that can be added to later as funds become available. Secondhand tools can sometimes be purchased cheaply but they are often not of a useful sweep or size, and in some cases have had the temper run out of them by over-enthusiastic grinding; this is sometimes difficult to detect. In general it will be found better to buy one good quality gouge than two or three doubtful secondhand tools for the same money. Remember that they may well be in use for the rest of your lifetime. Kits of tools are offered by most tool manufacturers but they often contain gouges which are seldom or never used, and the range of tools may not be suitable for the particular form of carving that you eventually choose. They are therefore a waste of money and it would be better at first to buy a few basic good quality gouges which can be added to as need, experience and finance dictate. Many of the great carvers were able to start with a block of wood marked out with a few rudimentary chalk or crayon lines and carve down to the required shape without recourse to measuring instruments or a method of carving. For lesser mortals, however, a disciplined method of carving means that unwanted wood can be confidently and quickly cut away, particularly in the early stages when the bulk of wood has to be removed. The method described in this book, and used for all the pages of designs, is called *blocking in.* It means that the work is carved in three separate phases: the *blocking in,* the *bosting in,* and the carving of the detail. Experience will eventually enable the carver to merge these phases together and in time to eliminate them completely. It is suggested, however, that this method is used initially, particularly for the early designs.

It is always a struggle to wrest one's first carving from a solid block of living wood, but the excitement and satisfaction with the end result are well worth all the effort involved. It is this first eager excitement that often produces an interesting carving, which is full of life instead of being 'static' and uninteresting. But as experience is gained and carvings become more complex it will be realised that a great deal of research needs to be done and a full understanding of the subject built up in order to design and carve a subject which looks right when finished. This leads the carver into fields which at first are difficult to imagine: from the legends and history of the great ships' figureheads, and the fascinating stories surrounding church carvings to the need to understand and appreciate, perhaps, the massive balanced beauty of the rhinoceros. There is so much inspiration wherever the carver travels that that first step of buying a few simple tools is the beginning of the road to a more visually exciting and satisfying world. I hope that the following pages will help in some way to guide you down that road.

1 The Woodcarver's Tools

BASIC TOOLS

Gouges and Chisels

All tools capable of removing wood are of use to the woodcarver, including engineers' tools such as drills, files, hacksaws, punches, etc. The bulk of all woodcarving, however, is carried out with the gouge, which is similar in appearance to the woodworker's or firmer chisel but from which it differs in two ways. The chisel is flat across its width whilst the gouge is rounded, and the chisel has the bevel ground on the top and the gouge at the bottom. The reason for the difference in the two tools is the way in which they are used – the chisel to pare comparatively small amounts of wood away down to an exact line, and the gouge to remove large quantities of wood by being pushed into the wood, either by hand pressure or by a blow from a mallet. The cutting edge slices cleanly down through the wood fibres, then the bevel, which is underneath, forces it out again leaving behind a spoon-shaped depression. If done correctly this not only removes a great deal of wood quickly and efficiently but also leaves behind a pleasing soft polish which is often left by carvers as a finish to their work.

Due to the vast number and complexity of woodcarving gouges and the need to make full use of those available it is important that the method by which they are identified is understood. Basically they are described in three ways:

1 The width across the gouge from tip to tip is measured in either imperial or metric measurements; the range, depending on the manufacturer, is usually from 1/16in (1.5mm) to 1in (25mm).

2 The curve (or sweep, to give it its correct name), is given a number ranging from No. 3, which is almost flat, to No. 11, which is just about U-shaped.

3 The gouge when viewed from the side is either straight, bent forwards (frontbent), or bent backwards (backbent). The same number of sweeps and widths are usually available in all three shapes.

When viewed from the top gouges can vary considerably in shape. The basic gouge, which it is suggested the beginner should start with, is straight along its length from the cutting edge to the tang. This gives a good strong tool that will take the impact of a heavy mallet and which, because it can be reground without losing its shape, will last a lifetime. All other shapes, such as spoon-bits, spades, fishtails, long alongee, short alongee, and so on, are wasted behind the cutting edge in a way generally suggested by their name, enabling the

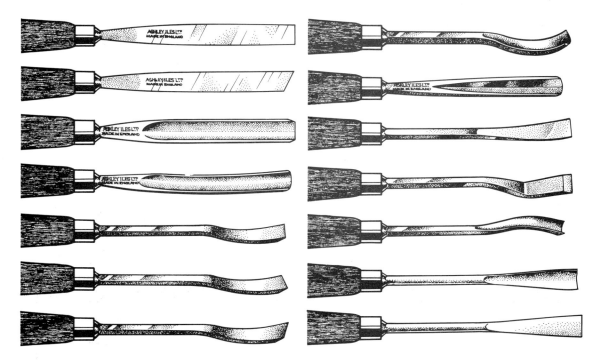

Fig 1 A selection of carving gouges. (By kind permission of Ashley Iles (Edge Tools) Ltd.)

carver to cut wood in places that would be inaccessible to the straight gouge. The fishtail in particular is a very pleasant tool to use. They all suffer, however, from the drawback of losing their shape when they are reground and from not having the strength of the straight gouge.

It has been stated that gouges have the bevel ground on the bottom and this is true of the vast majority of gouges. There are, however, a small number of gouges which have the bevel ground on the inside (*in-canal*). These are used by carvers who need to stab down vertically, for example when carving the vertical sides of raised lettering. For this purpose they are very

useful. The same operation can be carried out with the *out-canal*, although it needs to be held over at an angle to get a vertical cut, thus making it a little more difficult and time-consuming to use. It is suggested therefore that in-canal gouges should be avoided unless you contemplate doing a large amount of vertical stabbing down.

V or *parting tools* are in effect two firmer chisels welded together to form a V. They are used to carve incised lettering, the texturing of backgrounds by making a series of V cuts across them, and incised work where nearly all the work can be done with the V tool. They can be purchased straight or curved usually in three different angles:

10

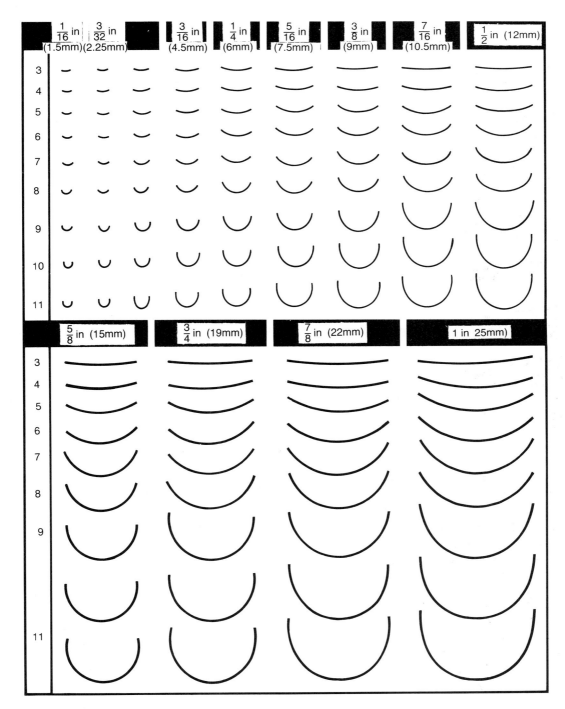

Fig 2(a)   Carving gouges are identified (a) by their width, (b) by the radius or
sweep, and (c) whether they are frontbent, backbent, or straight. Illustrated
above and overleaf are some available sweeps and sizes. (By kind permission of
Ashley Iles (Edge Tools) Ltd.)

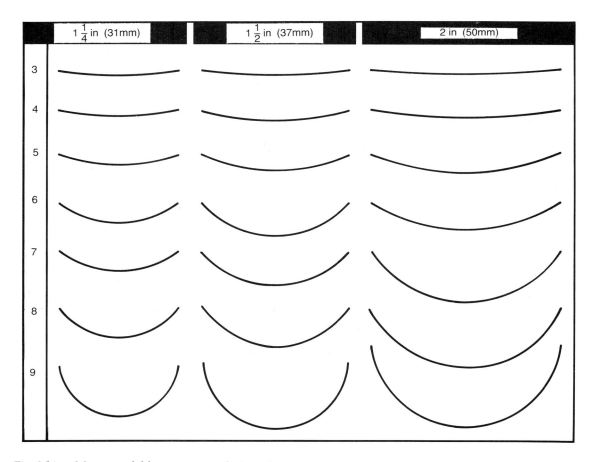

Fig 2(b)   More available sweeps and sizes for carving gouges.

45°, 60° and 90°. A recommended size and angle would be 3/8in (9mm) 60°. This tool will cope with most of the required work. A 3/16in (4.5mm) 60° would also be very useful.

The *maccaroni tool* has a flat bottom and vertical sides with the bevel ground on the inside. The *fluteroni* is similar except that it has a radius on the edges. The use of both these tools is very specialised and they should not be purchased unless a definite requirement is found for them.

Skew chisels, unlike the firmer chisels, are ground on both sides, the cutting edge being at an angle. They are mainly used for cleaning out corners.

Grounding tools are usually flattish gouges, about No. 3, with much less of a bend than the normal frontbent. They are used for levelling backgrounds especially, for example, when a relief has a raised border over which the gouge has to be worked. The same job can be done with a flattish, straight gouge (although with a little more difficulty), so the grounding tool should not be purchased initially.

A quick gouge is the term applied to a small U-shaped gouge, say a 10 or 11. This tool can penetrate more deeply into the wood before the tips enter so splitting the surface wood than a flatter gouge can. It is also called a *veiner* or *fluter* as it was once much in use for forming the veins and flutes on conventional acanthus foliage.

The Mallet

Another tool of particular use to the woodcarver is the carver's mallet which is round (as opposed to the carpenter's mallet which is square), and is usually turned from beech wood or lignum vitae. The beech mallet can give satisfactory service but the side grain tends to splinter quickly, and in order to provide the same weight and therefore force as the lignum vitae mallet it needs to be much larger. The lignum vitae mallet, however, is very much more expensive although in the long term this is a worthwhile outlay. Suitable mallets can be easily turned up on quite a small lathe provided care is taken not to overload the motor. Most hardwoods are suitable for the purpose although small blocks of lignum vitae, which is the ideal wood, can often be purchased from boat builders who use it to form self-lubricating bearings.

Scrapers

Scrapers are flat pieces of carbon steel which have had a lip formed on the edge by means of drawing the back of a gouge or similar tool along it at an angle. This lip provides the cutting edge. They are very efficient tools for cleaning up rough areas or removing gouge marks. They can also be used for a moderate amount of final shaping that would be difficult with gouges alone. The carver's scraper is shaped to provide a continuously changing curve which should fit any radius required. In practice, however, it has been found better to use a rectangular cabinet scraper which has had radii of different sizes ground on each corner. They can also be cut down with a hacksaw to make small scrapers with rounded ends which are ideal for cleaning up and shaping small difficult areas. They are inexpensive and a large number can be made up cheaply. It is often said that old saw blades can be ground up into scrapers but it is difficult to get a good edge on them. Broken glass also makes a good scraper but the edge quickly goes off and it can, of course, be dangerous.

Files

A selection of different shapes of engineer's files, both medium and coarse cut, are invaluable as they can not only be used for a moderate amount of shaping but will also quickly clean up a rough surface before final scraping and sanding takes place. Flat files are particularly useful for cleaning up flat surfaces such as the sides of bases, although they are often objected to on the grounds that they are not a carver's tool. The medieval carvers did not object to their use, however, and it is possible today to buy files the shapes of which were fashioned centuries ago. They are called *riffler files* and are shaped like an elongated figure 'S' and double-ended, the end shapes forming squares, flats, triangles, rounds, and so on. Where there is a choice it is better to choose those with a moderate curve as they are easier to use and just as versatile.

If one accepts the ethics of using files at all then the modern surform file can be of great value, particularly when rough shaping (or bosting in, as it is called) takes place – a large amount of wood can be quickly and smoothly removed, with the surface being left clean for pencil marks which are constantly being replaced. Of the three main surform blades the flat one is of little use to the carver but the round blade, fitted with a handle and with the front finger grip removed, is useful, as is the half round blade without a handle. The handle tends to get in the way on this blade as it is often convenient to pull instead of push it. Without the handle it is unsupported and therefore vulnerable to damage. This can easily be overcome by springing a piece of 1in (25mm) wide by 3/16in (4.5mm) wood between the end lugs that are normally used to hold the handle. Other surform blades are of limited use to the carver.

Carver's Punches

Carver's punches are available in a large variety of shapes including lettering. Their main use is for the texturing of backgrounds where a contrast is required between the main elements of the design and the background. They also have the effect of slightly bruising the wood which enables any stain or varnish which is used to penetrate more deeply so enhancing the contrast. They can also be used for decorative purposes such as on a horse's harness or round the edge of a gown. In most cases the decorative effect required can be pro-

duced by tapping the punch gently into the surface of the wood producing an embossed effect. It is sometimes useful, however, to have the punch marks raised above the surface of the wood, as in the case of lettering round the side of a plaque. This effect can be achieved with the punch by tapping it into the wood as before but then planing off the surface wood until the punch mark has almost disappeared. The application of a spot of boiling water to the compressed area of the punch mark will cause it to swell above the surrounding uncompressed wood. This will not produce a crisply-shaped letter, but can be used for a general raised pattern over an area. It has also been used to good effect to produce the veins that run across a horse's belly. There are many useful applications for this technique.

Using the punch is not perhaps as simple as may at first appear as it tends to sink more deeply into end grain and form a crisper shape than it does in side grain. It is easier if the punch is first tapped lightly whilst it is held vertically then again tapped lightly whilst it is held over at various angles in order to ensure that the corners of the mark are properly embossed. Where it has penetrated too deeply the application of a drop of boiling water to the punch mark will often restore it to about the right depth.

Chip Carving Knives

A sharp penknife will make a satisfactory chip carving knife but there are specialised knives on the market which give much greater control because of their shape. Some of them have different shaped blades that fit in a single handle. The Stanley slimknife can also be used for chip carving and is a very useful tool for general carving. For this purpose the Stanley blade No. 5905 will be found to be the most useful shape.

Routers

The hand router is still a useful tool although it has been largely superseded by the electric router. It is used to level backgrounds after the bulk of the wood has been removed with gouges and a grounding tool. They are still available and are reasonably priced but a good deal of practice is required to make full use of them.

The electric router is a very useful tool indeed for the carver. It will level backgrounds in reliefs much more quickly and accurately than can be achieved by hand. The use of moulding cutters or combinations of cutters, of which there is a large range of shapes and sizes, will enable the edges of bases, reliefs, nameboards, etc. to be attractively and quickly shaped, in some cases to be carved by hand later. The cutters are generally available in high speed steel or carbide-tipped. The latter, which last much longer, are very expensive indeed and are generally not worth the extra money for the very limited use given to them by the woodcarver.

Many router cutters have a small round projection on the bottom which

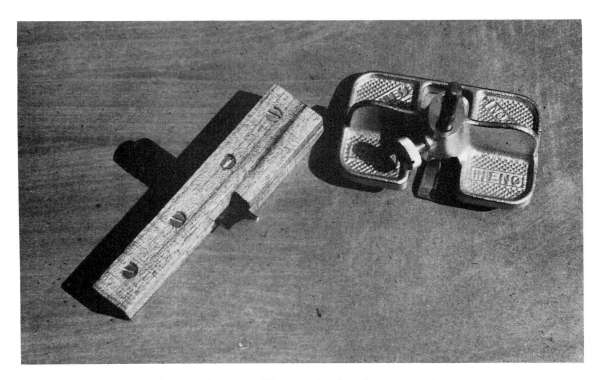

Fig 3 Scratch stock used to produce mouldings and a hand router used to level backgrounds.

guides the router along the edge of the wood thus enabling mouldings to be routed accurately without the danger of cutting in too far. They do, however, limit the depth of entry so that where possible cutters both with and without guides should be purchased. For the purposes of woodcarving most routers are hand-held so when making a choice it is as well to choose a router which can be easily handled and which has good visibility around the cutter. The bases of many routers almost enclose the cutter making it very difficult, for example, to see pencil marks at the end of a cut – it becomes easy to overshoot the mark. Some routers have a base which can be easily removed; in this case it is often possible to replace it with a perspex base which makes life much easier. An added refinement is to drill a series of holes about 1/8in (3mm) across the base from the centre to the perimeter at about 1/4in (6mm) intervals. this will enable small circles to be cut accurately if the hole is placed over a small nail driven into the centre of the circle in the wood and the router swung round it.

Special Tools

It is often found that the available tools are not sufficient or perhaps not quite the right shape to achieve the idea in the carver's mind. In many cases it is possible, easily and cheaply, to make up just the tool required to achieve that special effect. It is also very satisfying to produce just the right tool from pieces of waste material. The following examples will give some idea of what can be done with a little thought.

Nails or pieces of rod make excellent punches when the ends are filed to the correct shape. A nail with a rounded end will produce a very pleasant textured effect when tapped in at close intervals into the wood, or when the end is filed to a triangle or a square they can be

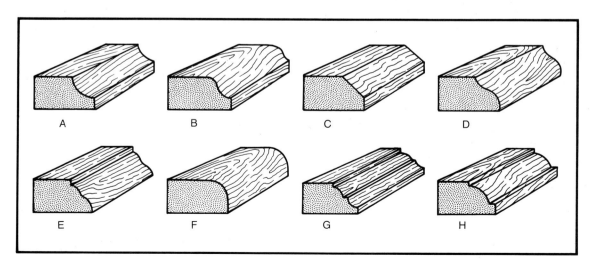

Fig 4 Router moulding cutter shapes suitable for forming decorative edges on name boards or round the bases of carvings.

effective in finishing the corners of reliefs when this is difficult with gouges alone. Although they are not generally as effective as a commercially produced scraper, old saw blades can be ground up to the shape required to clean up that difficult spot, or a short length of hacksaw blade glued with epoxy resin into a slot in the end of a length of rod will produce an effect like stitching in a horse's harness or a decorative edge to a gown when tapped lightly into the wood. Larger blades with more widely-spaced teeth can be used to texture small areas of wood. A length of rod with a shallow hole drilled in the end and fitted with a handle will produce a perfect sphere when pushed into the wood. This is useful for forming small eyes or a series of decorative marks.

The scratch stock has now been largely superseded by the router but it can still be a useful tool in producing small mouldings of a shape that is not available in commercial router cutters. It can be easily and quickly made up, the blade being ground up from a piece of old saw blade to the required shape. As with the scraper the lip formed by the grinding does the cutting. It is used by rubbing it backwards and forwards along the moulding after the bulk of the wood has first been removed with a gouge, the blade being tilted in the direction of cut. It automatically stops cutting when the full depth is reached.

CHOICE OF TOOLS

The bewildering number and shapes of woodcarving tools makes the choice of a tool kit a very difficult one especially as the tools required vary with the type of carving contemplated and the individual taste of the carver. The following suggested list is placed in order of importance, it being usual to start with the first three or four gouges, adding tools as experience and finance dictate.

5/8in (15mm) No. 7 straight.
3/8in (9mm) No. 10 straight.
3/8in (9mm) No. 6 straight.
1/4in (6mm) No. 11 straight.
3/8in (9mm) No. 3 straight.
1/4in (6mm) No. 3 straight.
1/8in (3mm) No. 3 straight.
1/8in (3mm) No. 11 straight.
3/8in (9mm) 60° V tool straight.
1/4in (6mm) frontbent spoonbit.
A two-sided bench oilstone 8×2×1in (203×50×25mm) medium and fine; various sized slipstones and leather strop.
Carver's mallet, round, preferably lignum vitae approx. 3in (75mm) diameter or a beechwood mallet about 11oz (320g).
A few cabinet scrapers of which one should have radii of different sizes ground on each corner, the others to be used for cutting to any shape required.
A variety of shapes and sizes of engineer's files, coarse and medium cut, and a set of riffler files.
A round surform blade with the handle but with the front finger grip removed, and a half round surform blade with no handle but a piece of 1×1/8in (25×3mm) wood sprung between the securing lugs to keep it rigid. This enables the blade to be either pushed or pulled.
A variety of carver's stamps.
A strong craft knife such as the Stanley slimknife fitted with the blade No. 5905, and/or a set of chip carving knives.

A hand router and, when the need arises, a made-up scratch stock.

Some carving operations can be both dusty and noisy, for example when sanding or routing, so the provision of paper dust masks, goggles, ear defenders, and, if the carver works in very heavy pieces of stock steel, capped boots, is a very wise precaution. They are rarely needed for any length of time but they could save an eye or one's hearing in the long run.

It is most important that all cutting tools should have their cutting edges protected, both for safety and to prevent damage to them. Canvas rolls are available commercially but the cut open top of a pair of rubber boots or a strip of car inner tube will do just as well with the tools pushed through slits cut in the rubber. For those who have a permanent workshop a convenient shelf with holes drilled in it to take the gouges will keep them safe and make them readily available. A dab of different coloured paint on each handle will immediately identify the required tool for those few fortunate enough to possess many gouges.

The bandsaw is a very desirable tool for the woodcarver, but few people have either the space or the finance for such a large machine, especially as one is required to cut up to 5in (125mm) of hardwood for it to be of any real value – anything much smaller would be a waste of money. The work can be carried out more laboriously and slowly by hand but a reasonable alternative is a professional quality jigsaw, with an orbiting as well as a reciprocating blade. These tools will readily cut to a depth of 2 1/2in (63mm), enabling 5in (125mm) to be cut

when the wood is approached from each side. It also has an advantage over the bandsaw in that it can make internal cuts after the wood has first been drilled to allow for entry of the saw blade.

A vice and other holding devices are essential and will be discussed later.

Sanding

In the main, any sanding required is carried out by hand. Drum sanders will quickly clean up flat surfaces such as the edges of bases, nameboards, and so on, and the sanding flapwheel, although more expensive, can be used to clean up carvings where hand sanding would be difficult. The fine-grade wheel in particular can be relied on not to sand over crisply carved edges if used with restraint.

WORKPLACE

There is normally very little choice of workplace, most carvers being sandwiched in between the lawnmower and the car in the garage. For those with a choice, a shed about 12ft × 6ft would be a reasonable size, fitted with a sturdy workbench of a comfortable height and as many cupboards and shelves as can be fitted in. If possible, the windows should face north to avoid the glare of the summer sun and an overhead transparent panel in the roof is also a great help. Artificial light is difficult to work in – a carving will look quite different in natural light. Neon tubes should be avoided where possible as they cast undesirable shadows and the stroboscopic effect of the tube can make some machinery, which is rotating

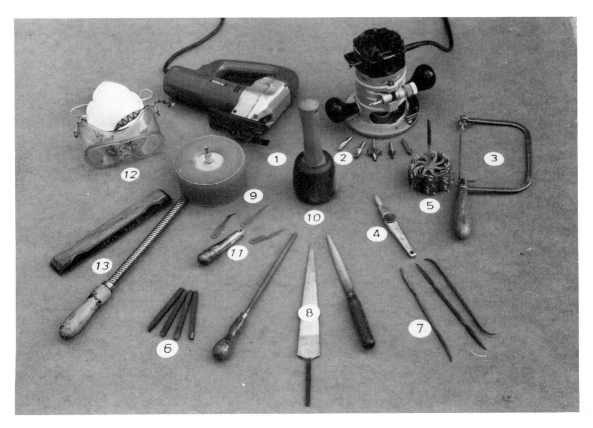

Fig 5 Additional tools of particular use to the woodcarver are: (1) electric jigsaw (2) electric router with a selection of router cutters (3) coping saw (4) Stanley slimknife (5) sanding flap-wheel (6) carver's punches (7) riffler files (8) various files (9) drum sander (10) carver's mallet (11) whittling or chip carving knives (12) safety equipment – mask and goggles (13) suitable surform blade shapes.

at about the same frequency, appear to slow up or even stop which is obviously dangerous. Strategically placed spotlights are probably the best solution.

For those confined to a limited area or those who like to sneak into the warmth of the kitchen during the winter a fold-up workmate bench is useful. There is a drawback in that they are usually too low for carving work but that can easily be overcome by attaching wooden blocks to the legs.

The preceding list of suggested tools is very comprehensive, so it is reassuring to know that a great deal of carving can be carried out with just a few well-chosen tools.

2 A Guide to Sharpening and Grinding

The need for a clean sharp cutting edge to woodcarving gouges is of the utmost importance for safety, accuracy and appearance. Sharpening can be a time-consuming job which is often avoided until it is too late. The result of this is ragged untidy work which then has to be sanded up by hand later, instead of the crisp clean cuts which look so well in the finished work and which are much quicker in the long run. Sharpening can be roughly divided into two parts: grinding and sharpening.

GRINDING

Grinding is used in the first place to produce the bevel on the gouge and later to renew the bevel after constant sharpening has altered its shape, or if the gouge edge has been gashed by it being dropped or perhaps hitting a nail in a piece of wood. It is carried out on either a hand-turned sandstone, turning in a trough filled with water, or a motor-driven grinding wheel. There is some discussion on which way the wheel should turn, away from or towards the operator. Both ways are effective but the wheel turning away from the operator, although removing less metal and therefore taking longer, produces less of a lip, or wire edge as it is called, and less heating, thus reducing the danger of running the temper out of the gouge. Of the two methods this one is probably the safest.

Sandstone wheels are difficult to obtain today having been superseded by the motor-driven grinding wheel. They do a good job, however, as long as they are kept trued up and the water in the trough is drained off after use as it tends to soften the stone. The motor-driven grindstone must be used with restraint, with the tool frequently being dipped in water as it is easy to overheat the gouge particularly when the edge is getting thin. It is also easy to run the temper out of the tool, which is indicated by a blue or straw colour at the tip. The only answer when this has happened is to grind away the tip until the colour has gone. This is both time-consuming and expensive.

The grinding angle varies with the type of gouge and the wood used. Soft deal requires a longer bevel to obtain a clean cut without tearing the wood than a hardwood which could cause the edge to crumble. For the same reason a small flattish gouge, used only for light work, would require a longer bevel than the obtuse bevel of a large bosting in gouge used mainly, say, in oak. It would be impractical to have gouges ground to all the required angles but a mean angle of 20° would be a good compromise, the small gouge being ground to about 15° and the heavy bosting in gouge to about 25°. Experience quickly indicates the best angle for any particular tool.

Gouges which have had the tips rounded to any marked degree or which have irregularly shaped cutting edges should first be squared up by presenting them flat on to the grinding wheel. Some carvers prefer to have a few of their gouges with rounded or convex cutting edges. This enables the centre of the gouge to enter the wood before the sides, making it easier for the gouge to slice cleanly and easily into the wood. These gouges are very pleasant to use but their use is limited and this method should be confined to a few special tools.

SHARPENING

To avoid overheating and the very rough edge produced by the grinding wheel the bevel is left thick at the tip. This thickness is then ground down by hand on an oilstone, so called because light machine oil is put on the stone before use in order to wash away the particles of metal ground off the gouge. These would otherwise clog the stone and render it useless. A useful size of stone is 8×2×1in (203×50×25mm). It is double sided with one side medium and the other coarse. The first problem is to decide the correct angle at which to hold the gouge on the stone. If the handle is held too high the edge will just be blunted and if held too low only the heel of the gouge and not the edge will be ground; both these things are easy to do. If, however, it is assumed that the gouge has been previously ground to the required angle then a slightly increased angle will be just about right for sharpening. This is easily ascertained by the use of the oil that has already been placed on the stone. If the cutting edge is placed just above the oil with the gouge lying along the stone then by lifting the handle the oil will squash out in front of the cutting edge just as it touches the stone. Lifting the gouge handle just a few degrees higher will give about the right sharpening angle.

The gouge now has to be rubbed across the stone to grind away the thickness of metal at the edge. This is done on the coarse side of the stone first, in one of two ways. Either it can be done by rubbing the gouge backwards and forwards in straight lines along the stone, imposing light pressure with the left hand near the gouge cutting edge and rotating the gouge backwards and forwards with the right hand to ensure that all the radius of the cutting edge is evenly ground. This method is simple to use but is slow and tends to wear grooves in the stone which then requires frequent and time-consuming dressing. Alternatively, the gouge can be rubbed across the whole surface of the stone in a figure of eight pattern, the handle being rotated backwards and forwards as before. This method is much quicker and reduces the problem of irregular wear on the stone. It is, however, more difficult to do. It is important with both methods that the gouge is not rocked up and down but kept at a constant height above the stone and that the whole radius of the cutting edge is evenly ground down. The very slight rounding of the tips that may occur by ensuring that the edge is ground right out to the tips will help to prevent the

 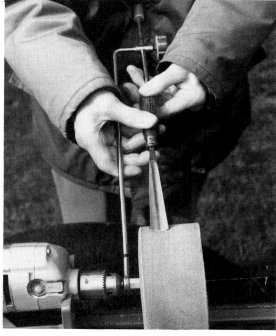

Fig 6 Sharpening guide – setting the sharpening angle by adjusting gouge cutting edge to line up with the marker line.

Fig 7 Support the knob on the end of the adjuster with the body.

surface wood splitting if the tips are inadvertently pushed below the surface of the wood. The radius of quick gouges or fluters (those with a U-shape, say a No. 10 or 11), is difficult to grind or sharpen with one movement of the wrist alone as with these gouges the bottom is rounded and the vertical sides are flat. It is better, therefore, to grind or sharpen these tools in three steps, the bottom first then each of the two sides.

It will be found that the thickness of the cutting edge can be easily seen as a line of light when it is viewed from the right angle. This enables progress to be checked and irregular grinding corrected as almost inevitably one part of the radius of the gouge will be ground down more than another. This is overcome by biasing the edge to grind down the thick areas.

It is often difficult to decide at what point to stop sharpening because if it is stopped too early the edge is still blunt and if too late the edge will crumble in use and become irregular. The easiest way to judge the right moment is to run a finger nail down the inside of the gouge. It will be found that as the metal has become thinner at the edge even the light pressure exerted by the left hand will have been sufficient to turn up the edge of the metal, forming a lip called the wire edge. When a well-defined wire edge has been formed evenly round the whole sweep of the gouge then it is sufficiently sharp. The wire edge then has to be removed with a slipstone. These are oblong stones of various sizes which have a radius formed on the two long edges, some stones having a sharp edge to fit the inside of V tools. A stone whose edge roughly fits the sweep of the tool is pushed down the inside of the gouge at a slight angle; this not only removes the wire edge but produces a slight bevel. This bevel is an advantage as it allows the tool to be used in an inverted position which is sometimes necessary. Some carvers produce very well defined bevels in this way. A slight wire edge will now have been formed on the other side of the cutting edge. This can be removed quickly with a few strokes with the flat side of the slipstone.

Once the gouge has been sharpened it is stropped on a leather strop that has been dressed with crocus powder mixed in a little vaseline. The tongues from an old pair of shoes are ideal for this purpose. The inside of the gouge can be stropped by rolling up the leather into a roll that will fit the inside of the gouge. A better alternative is to shape a piece of wood like a slipstone so the leather can be glued to this. The rounded edges are used for the inside of the gouge and the flat sides for the stropping. The finished gouge should slice through a piece of soft deal without tearing the wood and with the use of only moderate hand pressure.

It is possible to buy kidney-shaped oilstones which are also cone-shaped. One side is convex and the other concave so they will sharpen both the inside and outside of gouges. The technique is similar to that already described for flat oilstones.

Tools used on hardwoods such as oak, or gritty woods like teak, quickly lose their keen edge. This can be restored with the strop which should be constantly on hand for this purpose. It is some time before a recourse to the oilstone becomes necessary. Another method of restoring a dull edge is with a piece of slipstone-shaped wood which has had a piece of fine-grade emery cloth glued to it and is used in the same way as the slipstone. Perhaps the quickest way of all is to buff the edge of the tool on a buffing wheel that has been dressed with a fine-grade buffing compound. The wheel will spread to take up the shape of the gouge edge but this method should be used with the greatest restraint as a few seconds too long will result in the edge being dulled.

Scrapers

Scrapers are sharpened by placing them in a vice and filing the edges at right angles with a fine file. The resulting burr on the edge is then filed off with the same file held flat against the scraper to avoid the slightest bevel on the edge. The back of a gouge or similar tool is then drawn along each edge at a slight angle with as much force as possible to produce the sharp lip that does the cutting. Special steels can be purchased to form the lip but the back of a gouge is quite effective. It is difficult to produce cutting edges on small scrapers but as these are used mainly for cleaning up and shaping places it is unnecessary. For a gouge it is usually sufficient to leave the lip formed by the initial filing. This normally produces acceptable results.

When purchasing scrapers it is advisable to choose the thinnest available. These are often avoided by the cabinet maker as they quickly heat up and burn the fingers but this is not a problem for the carver as the area to be scraped is usually quite small. The ability to bend a scraper slightly between the fingers is useful as it gives a better cut, particularly when it is pushed diagonally over the wood instead of in straight lines.

CARVING GOUGE GRINDING AND SHARPENING GUIDE

The foregoing method described for grinding and sharpening woodcarving gouges is traditional and has stood the test of time. If properly carried out it always produces a clean sharp edge. It does, however, rely on the skill of the operator to maintain the gouge handle at a constant height above the stone in order to avoid a rounded edge and also to produce the correct bevel angle. It is also both laborious and time-consuming.

The guide avoids these problems and in addition provides a hollow ground edge which can be honed up more effectively than a flat one. It does have the drawback that without care the temper can be run out of the gouge by overheating. This is easily overcome by frequent dousing in cold water and restraint when the gouge cutting edge is offered up to the grinding wheel.

The guide has been designed for use with a horizontally-clamped power drill and a 5in (128mm) drum sander. Both these tools are probably available in the average household but the sanding belts, commercially available for the drum sander, are rather too coarse for the final finishing and the foam rubber tends to spin out of balance. Where possible it would be better to take the extra time to construct the sanding wheel described below, but quite a good job can be done with the drum, especially if finer grit belts are made up for the job by the carver.

Construction

Provided that the measurements and angle shown in the drawing are adhered to, the guide can be made up from any material available to the carver in the bits box. The following design, which works well in practice, is simple to construct and makes use of readily available materials.

Materials required:
28in (711mm) of 1/4in (6mm) rod
1in (25mm) of 1/2in (12mm) rod
1 × 1/4in bolt, preferably whit

Cut from the 1/4in (6mm) rod two lengths 3 1/4in (82mm) and 7 1/2in (190mm). Heat the end of the remaining rod to a red heat and bend it round a length of 1/4in (6mm) rod to form a circle which will become the bearing. This can be done cold but with more difficulty. Bend the other end of the rod to a right angle 14in (350mm) from the bearing centre ensuring that it is also at right angles to the vertical line of the bearing. This end of the rod must then be cut down to a length which will bring the adjuster rod in line with the centre of the sanding drum. This will depend on whether a 2 1/2in (64mm) sanding drum or a made up 1 1/2in (35mm) wooden drum is used.

Drill a 1/4in (6mm) hole through the

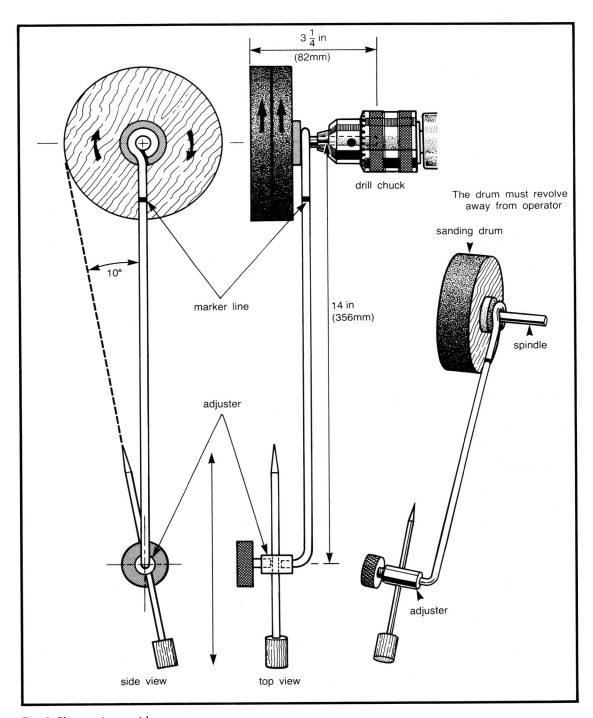

Fig 8 Sharpening guide.

centre of the piece of 1in (25mm) rod to take the adjuster rod and drill a tapping size hole through the length of the rod in preparation for tapping it to take the 1/4in whit bolt. Drill out half of this hole with a 1/4in (6mm) drill. The right angle bend of the 14in (350mm) rod can now be entered into the hole just drilled and the 1in (25mm) rod turned until the adjuster hole is pointing at a 10° angle to the 14×1/4in (350×6mm) rod. Now solder it into this position.

Grind one end of the 7 1/2in (190mm) adjuster rod to a point and glue, with an epoxy resin glue, a short length of 3/4in (19mm) dowel on the other end after first drilling it half-way through with a 1/4in (6mm) drill to take the rod.

Tap the tapping size hole in the 1×1/2in (25×12mm) rod with a 1/4in whit tap and screw in the 1/4in (6mm) bolt. This should now securely hold the adjuster rod in position when tightened up.

The marker line is formed by means of a shallow hacksaw cut which has had black paint rubbed into it. It should be approximately 1 1/4in (32mm) from the bearing centre. This measurement is not critical as the marker line is only used as a guide, the cutting edge being adjusted to either just before or just after the marker line depending on the length of bevel required by the carver.

Using the Guide

Caution: THE DRUM MUST REVOLVE AWAY FROM THE OPERATOR

Drill a small hole in the top centre of the handle of the gouge to be sharpened and locate the pointed end of the adjus-ter in the hole. Then with the gouge angled over the marker line adjust the adjuster until the gouge cutting edge lines up with the marker line (see Fig 6). When the gouge edge is swung back to the centre of the sander drum the bevel should be at the desired grinding angle of about 20° in relation to the sanding drum. Support the knob on the end of the adjuster with the body as in Fig 7 and with the drum rotating move the gouge cutting edge backwards and forwards on the abrasive surface with the right hand, whilst supporting the gouge with the left hand, ensuring that it remains located in the pointed end of the adjuster. Immerse the tool frequently in cold water. The cutting edge can be checked for even grinding by holding the gouge at an angle to the light source. The thickness of the metal will show as a line of light when the correct angle is found. Once the tool has been sufficiently ground, as indicated by a well-defined wire edge, the process is repeated by changing to a fine sander belt in the case of the drum sander or angling the gouge towards the fine grit band in the case of the made-up wooden drum.

Once grinding and sharpening are complete the wire edges can be removed with a slipstone, and the gouge stropped both inside and out with a leather strop.

THE SANDING DRUM

The sanding drum is turned from a piece of 1 1/2in (37mm) wood or better still two 3/4in (19mm) pieces glued together with the grain running at right angles to each other. For those without a lathe the two 5in (128mm) circles can be cut out with a coping saw. Any irregularities can be trued up later by scraping with a chisel once the drum is rotating in the drill.

The remaining 3 1/4in (82mm) piece of rod is used for the drum spindle. Drill a small hole, about 1/6in (1.5mm), through the end of the rod about 3/16in (4.5mm) from the end. Tap in a small nail after first removing the head. Drill the drum centre with a 1/4in (6mm) drill and make a chisel cut across one end of the drilled hole. This enables the nail to sink into the drum when the spindle which has been first coated with epoxy resin is tapped home. The nail prevents the spindle rotating inside the drum. Alternatively Black and Decker produce a spindle intended for use with electric drills. In this case the centre hole should be drilled out 1/2in (12mm). Cut a 1 1/2in (37mm) disc from a piece of 1/4in (6mm) wood and drill the centre 1/4in (6mm). Slip it over the drum spindle and glue it to the drum to form a spigot that will prevent the guide fouling the perimeter of the drum when it is revolving.

The guide is intended for sharpening and grinding straight gouges, but it can also be used to sharpen frontbent and backbent gouges. In this case the marker line cannot be used to set the correct grinding angle. Instead the pointed end of the adjuster rod is located in the small hole drilled in the end of the gouge handle as before and the cutting edge laid on the abrasive. By viewing it from the side it is possible to position the bevel at about the right angle. A further refining adjustment can be made after the tool has been ground for a short time.

3 Woods and their Storage

Wood is classified into two main groups, soft and hard, with the hardwood coming from deciduous trees and the softwood from coniferous trees. This is an unsatisfactory classification for the woodcarver as many so-called hardwoods are softer than softwoods. For example, balsa, which is classified as a hardwood, is extremely soft and Parana pine, classified as a softwood, is quite hard enough to be used for treads in staircases. There is no satisfactory way of determining the suitability of wood for carving other than experience, although pressing a thumbnail into the wood with as much force as possible will give some slight indication of its hardness.

Although it would be very pleasant to have a vast range of woods to choose from, in practice, because most woods are converted to a small size before sale, the comparatively large blocks required by the carver are rarely commercially available except through specialist suppliers. Offcuts of a fairly large size can often be purchased cheaply from wood merchants because they contain a split or some other fault which can be carved round by the carver. Alternatively saw mills will cut blocks to order. These are generally green but can be quickly and cheaply dried out in a kiln, the dried wood being quite satisfactory for carving. If space is available wood can be dried out in the air but this will take about one year for every inch of thickness of the wood, depending on the conditions.

Where a choice of wood is available to the carver it is as well to consider the characteristics of each wood and the type of carving for which it is required before making a choice. For example will it carve well, stand well outside in the elements, take a good finish? Can fine detail be carved into it? Will it stain or fume successfully? Does it warp or split badly? Would its grain detract from the detail in the carving? Has it a good colour and figuring? Is it scented? Will it affect the flavour of food? Does it glue up satisfactorily? To summarise all the available woods would be impossible but a few of the more readily available are discussed in the following list.

English oak was widely used by the medieval carvers many of whose robust carvings survive to this day. It has a pleasing light, yellow-brown colour when first cut turning to a dark brown with age. The grain is attractive without being obtrusive, particularly if the logs are quarter-sawn to show off the medullary rays. It is, however, open-grained which makes it unsuitable for carving fine detail and it tends to split even after the carving is commenced and when it has been properly seasoned. It finishes well with all forms of finish and the heart wood can be successfully fumed.

Turkey oak is very similar to English oak but the grain tends to be wilder.

Jap oak carves cleanly but is difficult to obtain in any size.

Chestnut is similar in appearance to oak. It is sometimes called coffin oak from the practice in the past of some coffin makers substituting the cheaper chestnut for oak from which it is almost indistinguishable. The medullary rays are, however, much less conspicuous and the wood is softer. It carves well but like oak is open-grained and therefore not suitable for detailed work. It will fume well.

Lime (linden) is a creamy white wood with little figuring, known in America as 'basswood' and used extensively by Grinling Gibbons for his remarkably detailed carvings. Probably the best of all carving woods, it is ideal for detail and relief work where a distinctive grain would detract from the detail.

Elm is a tough, sinewy, medium-brown wood with a fine but unobtrusive grain. It is hard and tough enough for carving slender sections that could not be attempted in most other woods, such as the legs of a race-horse. It is also close grained enough to take a reasonable amount of detail. It finishes well, is durable, especially in water, and was once used for the slats of water wheels. English elm is generally lighter in colour than Cornish elm and has fewer knots. It is a good compromise wood allowing all forms of carving to be undertaken with confidence.

Teak carves well but has a gritty grain which quickly takes the edge off gouges. It is very expensive indeed although the great beauty of the wood probably makes the extra expense worth while. It is difficult to glue up due to the large amount of oil contained in the wood although the oil does protect the wood making it durable for outside. A cheaper but less attractive alternative is **Iroko bastard teak,** which looks very well when freshly carved but quickly changes to a dark brown overall shade which tends to conceal the grain.

Jarrah is an Australian wood similar in appearance to mahogany for which it is often mistaken; carves and finishes well and is highly resistant to water.

Mahogany is available in a vast range of reds ranging from deep red to the very attractive reddish-brown of Brazilian mahogany. They all carve cleanly although some tend to split and they all finish well.

Fruit woods (pear, apple, cherry and so on) mainly carve well and will take fine detail. They are difficult to obtain in any size but are well worth saving and drying for small carvings.

Hornbeam is a pleasant carving wood, once extensively used for coppicing.

Ash is a handsome wood which carves well. It is a very light wood with a distinctive grain, ideal where grain is required to complement and enhance a carving, such as in an abstract or a torso.

Boxwood, now difficult to obtain in any size, is light yellow in colour with little or no grain. It finishes well and will take a very fine detail.

Yellow pine is straight-grained and knot-free and was once used extensively for carving the great ships' figureheads. It glues up well, carves cleanly and is resistant to water.

Jelutong is a cheaper alternative to yellow pine and is used for much the same purpose. It carves well but tends to splinter, so very sharp tools with long bevels are required.

Sycamore is a hard white wood which carves cleanly although it tends to take the edge off gouges due to a gritty grain.

Holly is a dense, very white wood with little grain and is ideal for inlay work and all forms of carving.

Walnut is a most attractive wood which carves well. It is difficult to obtain as most of it is used for veneer work. Quite large offcuts are, however, sometimes available.

Lignum vitae is the world's heaviest known wood. The colour varies from chocolate brown to yellow tinged with green. It is a very beautiful wood but not suitable for the beginner due to its hardness. It is difficult to obtain, although offcuts are quite often available from boat builders who use it for self-lubricating bearings. It is ideal for turning carvers' mallets where its great weight enables the mallet to be smaller in size than would be possible with a lighter wood.

Greenheart is a pleasant carving wood. Very resistant to water, it is often used for the piles of jettys and to make fishing rods. It is occasionally available in large blocks when jettys are dismantled and is often in good condition after many years of immersion.

Parana pine is an attractive, light brown wood streaked with red and yellow. Carves well but tends to splinter and is one of the few commercial woods cut to a width of 10in (25cm), the width of stair treads for which it is widely used.

FAULTS IN WOOD

Wood is a superbly beautiful and natural medium in which to work. It does, however, possess faults which the carver needs to understand in order to avoid or at least reduce them and perhaps even at times turn them to advantage. The main problem is splitting, or 'shakes'.

1 The wood at the ends of a plank is more exposed to the air so it dries out before the centre of the plank. The end wood tries to shrink but is prevented from doing so by the still wet centre wood, and the resulting tension causes the ends to shake. This effect can be reduced by liberally coating the ends of the plank with paint or paraffin wax to slow up the drying out process. It is also a good idea to obtain the planks a little longer than actually required so that the surplus wood can be cut away if shakes develop.

2 The annual rings are formed by the difference in growth and wetness of the

early wet spring wood and the drier late summer wood. The resultant uneven drying out between the rings and the consequent tensions set up in the wood cause the plank to shake. The shakes this time extend the full length of the plank and this also causes the plank to curve across its width in the opposite direction to the curve of the annual rings. This effect can be reduced, if not eliminated, by gradual drying out in a well-ventilated place. The air is allowed to flow freely between the planks by placing spacers between them, the weight of one plank on top of the other will also help to prevent the curl. If, after all precautions have been taken, the wood does curl, it can often be straightened out by using it for a relief. The relief is carved on the convex side of the curl because wood tends to curl towards the relieved side. Indeed, when carving on a perfectly flat piece of wood it is often necessary to relieve the other side to prevent curling.

3 Wood, particularly oak, however well seasoned, will sometimes shake after the carving has commenced. This is due to the tensions which already exist in the wood being released by the carver as he slices through the wood fibres. There is no remedy for this although these shakes do tend to close up once the tensions have been released. For this reason it is important that the shake is filled with beeswax rather than wood or plastic wood, as the wax will eventually squeeze out allowing the shake to close, whereas wood will prevent closure causing the shake to appear elsewhere. The beeswax will also prevent the edges of the shake crumbling when the wood is sliced through.

4 'Thundershakes' are so called because they usually occur in the violent thunderstorms that are a regular feature of tropical weather. They are caused by the wind bending the trees over and causing the rupture of the wood fibres, particularly of young saplings. The wood cells continue to grow around the fault but it is always present and forms a weakness in the wood. If the plank is given a sharp tap on the floor it will shatter where it has been damaged.

Wood that has been lying in the forest for many years can still be quite sound. Indeed many tropical countries store their wood in water by forming rafts in lakes or the sea-shore, and it was once a common practice to leave green planks in a running stream to wash the sap out of them. Where water has penetrated, though, rot could have set in which is not always easy to detect. The plank should produce a sharp sound, almost a ring, when tapped instead of the dull thud that would indicate the presence of rot. Some woods, such as beech, can be attractively stained by the ingress of water and, provided they are sound, will carve and look well when finished.

STORING WOOD

Wood should be stored horizontally with the air being allowed to flow through by placing spacers between the planks. It should be kept in a dry, and most importantly, sun-free place with all the ends being liberally coated with paint or paraffin wax. Large baulks of wood can be successfully stored upright as they are unlikely to sag and it will be found easier to handle them.

4 Vices, Cramps and the Universal Joint

The ability to hold wood safely and securely, particularly as the work proceeds and crisply carved edges become vulnerable to damage, is of the utmost importance. Therefore both for the sake of safety and accuracy consideration must be given as to how the work will be held from the outset. In many cases it will be found possible to make up holding devices easily and quickly from bits of spare stock although a few basic cramps will also be invaluable.

VICES

Vices are available in two main types, the woodworker's and the engineer's vice. Both are suitable although the engineer's stands higher and is more versatile in the home workshop as it can be used for both woodworking and metalworking projects. One with 4in (100mm) jaws is about the right size, preferably fitted with a quick release mechanism which saves the seemingly endless job of screwing and unscrewing every time the work needs to be moved in the jaws.

When the carving is first designed it may well be possible to leave a block of wood on the bottom which will allow the work to be held in the vice and which can be sawn off when the carving is complete. Alternatively, a block of wood can be screwed or glued to the bottom of the carving. The block should be square to save the necessity of opening and closing the vice jaws every time the carving is turned through 90°, and it should be about 4in (100mm) long to allow the work to be not only turned but angled over to get at the difficult parts of the carving. When screw holes would be undesirable in the bottom of the base the block can be glued on with newspaper sandwiched in between it and the base. This will hold the work securely enough, the block being easily prised off later when the carving is complete.

THE SANDBAG

With a carving held rigidly in a vice the slender legs of a race-horse, for example, would be vulnerable to damage if some heavy bosting in blows (roughing out) were required at the top of the work. In this case a bag about 18×18in (45×45cm) should be made up from strong canvas and partially filled with a mixture of dry builders sand and sawdust. This will support the carving overall when it is bedded down into the bag. Where the carving is irregular it is possible to shake the contents of the bag down to one end to fit the irregularities.

CRAMPS

A few G cramps of different sizes are a useful addition to the tool kit as they possess great strength and considerable pressure can be achieved with them. The depth of throat, however, is rarely sufficient for the size of cramp needed and the time taken to adjust them is lengthy. An alternative is the sliding cramp which, although less robust, has a larger throat and can be quickly adjusted. It can even be fitted in position with one hand if you need the other.

Threaded Rod

Where very large work is contemplated, such as a ship's figurehead, and the wood is first glued up to roughly the shape of the finished work, it is possible to use sash cramps for the cramping up. However, they are expensive and have little depth of throat, making the cramping of irregular shaped work difficult. A much cheaper and more effective method of cramping in this case is to use lengths of rod threaded throughout its length and about 5/8in (15mm) diameter, preferably with a whitworth thread. Two pieces of 2×2in (50×50mm) wood with a 5/8in (15mm) hole in each end are positioned over the two pieces of rod. The work is then sandwiched between them. Considerable pressure can be exerted in this way when the nuts are tightened up. The cramp can be made infinitely variable by altering the lengths of the 2×2in (50×50mm) wood or by screwing the dividing nuts halfway on to their thread and then screwing a further length of rod into the other half of the nut (Fig 9).

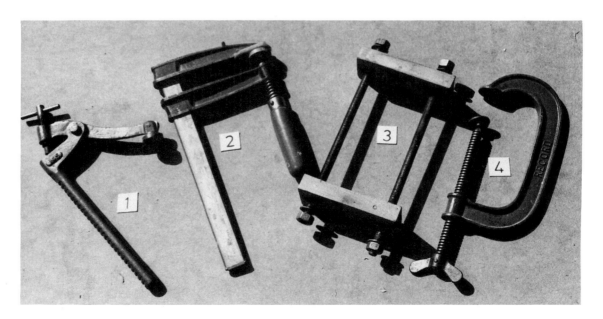

Fig 9 Various cramps: (1) bench holdfast (2) sliding cramp (3) 5/8in (15mm) threaded rod (4) G cramps.

Bench Holdfast

It is occasionally useful to be able to cramp a work in the middle of the work bench where it is not possible to use the edge of the bench for G cramps. In this case the bench holdfast can be used. It is quickly adjustable but does require the work bench top to be drilled through to take the socket into which the holdfast fits. This is a permanent fitting which lies flush and does not detract from the normal use of the bench. There are generally two sizes available, the larger one being much more versatile and worth the extra expense (Fig 9).

The Carver's Screw

The carver's screw is a length of threaded rod, pointed at one end, with a large butterfly nut on the other end. The pointed end is screwed into a pre-drilled hole in the bottom of the carving and the screw is then passed through a hole in the bench or carver's stand. The work is thus held rigid when the butterfly nut is tightened. It is mainly used for large work but it has the drawback that a large hole has to be drilled in the bottom of the carving. It also does not allow the work to be tilted over at an angle so its use is limited.

HOLDING RELIEF WORK

It is quite possible to hold a relief with sliding or G cramps but they are inconvenient as the cramp needs to be constantly moved because it is invariably in the position needed to be worked on. They can also damage a gouge edge if accidentally hit by the carver. It is possible to cramp a relief with made-up wooden buttons which rest on the edge of the work, the other end being screwed to the bench. Although this overcomes the possible damage to the gouge edge they do still tend to get in the way.

A simply made-up alternative, which overcomes both these problems, is the peg board which consists of a piece of 18×18×1/2in (452×452×12mm) plywood which has had a series of 1/2in (12mm) holes drilled in it at about 1 1/2in (37mm) intervals. The pegs are made up from 1 1/2in (37mm) lengths of wood dowel 3/4in (19mm) diameter, with 1in (25mm) being wasted down to 1/2in (12mm) either on a lathe or by hand filing. When two of the pegs are placed in suitably positioned holes in the board the relief can be positioned against them and a further two pegs placed on the other side of the relief and adjacent to it. Two wedges opposing each other are forced in between the relief and the pegs to hold the work securely. A square block of wood approximately 4×4×1 1/2in (102×102×37mm) should be glued to or screwed to the bottom of the peg board to enable it to be held in the vice and when necessary turned round in 90° stages (Fig 10).

A worthwhile refinement to this, which enables the peg board to be turned freely whenever the vice is slackened, is a simple swivelling joint. This enables the board to be used both for relief work and as a table of a convenient height for working on small pieces of inlay or clay modelling. The joint is constructed in two main parts: firstly, a piece of 3in (75mm) dowel, about 4in (100mm) long with a saw cut in one end, is positioned in a 3in (75mm) hole drilled in the centre of a piece of

Fig 10 Peg board with swivel, used to hold a relief when G clamps would obstruct the carving.

Fig 11 Inverted peg board showing the swivel sectioned.

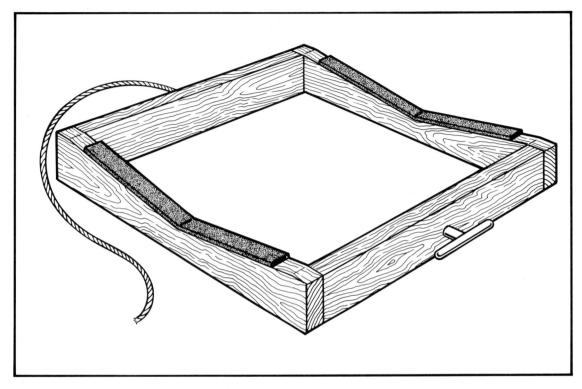

Fig 12 V frame used to hold heavy, irregularly shaped carvings such as ships' figureheads.

3×4×1 1/4in (75×102×31mm) wood. A wedge is then glued and driven into the sawcut to secure the two together. Secondly a block of hardwood 4×4×4in (102×102×102mm) then has a 3in (75mm) hole drilled in the centre of it and is then sawn in half down the centre of the hole. When the two halves are placed in the vice and the 3in (75mm) dowel positioned in the centre hole the two halves will clamp on to the dowel when the vice is tightened up and prevent it turning, or allow it to turn when the vice is just slackened off slightly. To prevent the two halves coming apart when they are removed from the vice they can be held together with two 1/4in (6mm) bolts which must be recessed well into the blocks to prevent the vice jaws catching them when it is tightened. The bolts should be tightened just sufficiently to hold the two halves of the swivel together. The sides of the two halves of the blocks should be recessed approximately 1/4in (6mm) to take the jaws of the vice. This will prevent the swivel slipping out of the jaws when the vice is slackened off.

The 3×4×1 1/4in (75×102×31mm) block is then screwed and glued to the bottom of the peg board. Confused by all this? Have a look at Figs 10 and 11.

LARGE WORK

Large work is usually of sufficient weight to make clamping unnecessary. When it is round, however, or very irregular in shape it can need fixing in position. This can be done by constructing a frame about 18in (457mm) square from 3×2in (75×50mm) wood, two sides of the frame having long shallow V cuts made in them. When the carving is laid in the V cuts this will normally be sufficient to hold it securely. If further fixing is required a piece of stout cord, secured to one side of the frame, drawn across the carving and secured to a cleat the other side, will hold the work firmly. Damage to the edges of the carving will be prevented if strips of carpet or carpet felt are glued to the edges of the two V cuts (see Fig 12).

The V Board

It can be difficult to hold an irregularly-shaped piece of wood so the sides can be cleaned up with a plane for marking out. Clamps would get in the way of the plane. A piece of 18in (457mm) square 1/2in (12mm) plywood, with two strips of wood glued and screwed to it to form a V, will wedge the wood in place sufficiently firmly for it to be planed (see Fig 13).

THE UNIVERSAL JOINT

The simple wood block secured to the bottom of the carving is an excellent way to hold work in the vice. A universal joint, however, gives the carver much more freedom because the work can be

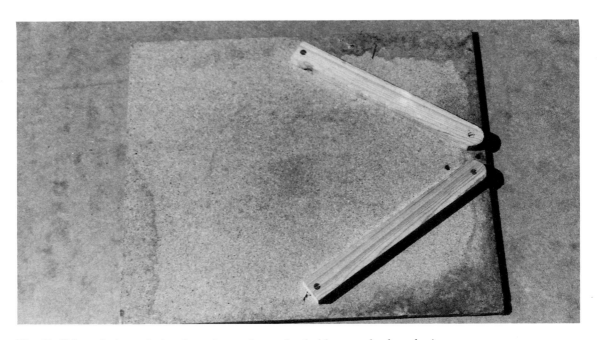

Fig 13 V board: irregularly shaped wood can be held securely for planing when wedged in the V.

Fig 14 Universal joint: this will enable a carving to be held securely, turned and angled over when screwed to the bottom of the base carving.

moved quickly and easily to any position required and saves the necessity of constantly moving round the carving in order to view it from all angles, which is vital to achieve a balanced work. The universal joint described here has been in use for many years and has proved quite satisfactory. It is used in a vice with 4in (100mm) jaws which are large enough to permit the joint to be of sufficiently robust construction to take heavy bosting in blows. It must be made from a tough hardwood, such as elm or oak, and is constructed in three main parts – a ball and two blocks. The ball is about 3in (77mm) in diameter and is turned from a piece of 3×5in (77×127mm) hardwood. A spigot is left on one end 1 3/4in (45mm) diameter. The spigot has a saw cut in the end and is entered into a 1 3/4in (45mm)

hole drilled through the centre of a piece of 4×3×1in (102×77×25mm) wood. A glued wedge is then driven firmly into the saw cut to hold the two together. The two blocks are 5×4×2in (127×102×50mm) each with a 3in (77mm) diameter circle scribed on the side of each block, the circumference being 3/8in (9mm) down from the edge of the block. The two circles are hollowed out with gouges to form the socket which will take the ball. They are first drilled with a small hole in the centre of each circle to indicate the correct depth of 1 1/2in (37mm) to which to carve. The final stages of the gouging out of the sockets will be made easier by covering the ball with chalk and rotating it in the two sockets. This shows up the high spots which can then be removed with the gouge.

Fig 15 Universal joint sectioned.

The assembled ball and socket will now give a limited universal movement. If wood 1 3/4in (45mm) wide is now removed from the sockets down to the full depth of the ball each side of the spigot, the spigot will be able to move over to the full 90° position.

The blocks are recessed by about 1/4in (6mm) on each side to take the jaws of the vice. This prevents the work falling out of the jaws when the vice is slackened off to change the position of the carving.

A 1/4in (6mm) recess cut under the blocks to accept the central bar of the vice will also help to locate them. The edges of the blocks are chamfered in order to prevent the piece of 4×3×1in (102×77×25mm) wood from fouling them when the work is angled over. It is undesirable to secure the two blocks together with bolts, as in the case of the peg board swivel, as it is often required to remove the work from the vice and lie it on the sandbag for bosting in. In this case the blocks would form an obstruction.

To use the universal joint, the piece of 4×3×1in (102×77×25mm) wood which is secured to the top of the spigot is screwed to the bottom of the carving. If screw holes are undesirable, a piece of wood of the same dimensions is glued to the base of the carving, with newspaper sandwiched in between and the joint screwed to this. It is a simple matter when the carving is complete to prise off the block.

5 Wood Finishes and Repairs

The simplest and probably the most effective method of finishing a carving is just to leave the gouge marks in the wood. If razor-sharp tools have been used, and care taken with each cut, the polish left by the back of the gouge bevel, rubbed vigorously with wood shavings or clean straw, will look very well – indeed, most of the medieval carvers left their work in this condition. However, the surface of wood that has been left unprotected in this way quickly becomes ingrained with dirt which conceals both the colour and grain. The open wood pores also allow the ingress and regress of water vapour, which is a possible cause of future shakes.

SMOOTH POLISHED FINISHING

There are a great many possible finishes, some of which leave the wood with its natural look and yet still provide protection from dirt. It is true to say, though, that all finishes darken the wood to a greater or lesser extent.

Where a smooth polished finish is required it is as well to keep the carving cleaned up with scrapers, or pieces of broken glass and files, as the work proceeds. This not only saves time at the end but enables the work to be easily and accurately marked out when required. The final stages of the smoothing are carried out with reducing grades of sandpaper, finishing with flour paper. The wood dust can be removed by a very vigorous rubbing with a clean rag dipped in white spirit, or a tac rag which is commercially available. This vigorous rubbing not only removes the dust but imparts a burnished glow to the wood, and this makes a good surface for the wax or varnish to be applied later.

Open-grained woods such as oak should have a grain filler of the appropriate colour rubbed into the grain before the sanding starts. When sanding starts, rough areas which had not been visible before become obvious. It is rarely poss ible to sand these out with sandpaper alone so recourse should be made to the scrapers and files, or recutting with gouges, to clean these up. It is sometimes necessary to use strips of sandpaper pulled back and forth with two hands to sand certain shapes. Used like this the sandpaper can keep breaking, but sticky tape or masking tape stuck to the back of the strip will overcome this.

WAX POLISHING

A proprietary wax polish or shredded beeswax melted down in turpentine to a smooth paste will provide most woods with a lovely soft lustre when frequently applied and polished up with a soft duster. Unfortunately, like the plain gouge finish, the surface is unprotected and quickly becomes dirty. An acceptable compromise is first to apply varnish or sanding sealer to the smoothed wood, including the bottom of the carving, then to rub it down when dry with well-worn flour paper, using steel wool (0 grade) for the areas that prove difficult to sand. When the wax polish is applied after this and polished up, the finish will provide the protection of the varnish and the lovely soft lustre of wax. Any slight damage to the finish afterwards is easily restored with steel wool, dipped in wax polish and vigorously rubbed over the damaged area.

Beeswax

Occasionally soft knots are found in the wood after the carving has commenced. These have to be removed, leaving a hole, or shakes will form due to the release of tensions in the wood. These should be filled in with beeswax of a suitable colour, the natural variation in the colour of beeswax giving a wide choice of colours. Alternatively it can be stained by melting the wax over a low heat and adding a little wood stain of the desired colour. Any wax that then squeezes out when the shake closes can be pared off with a sharp knife.

STAINS

There is an almost endless list of wood stain recipes which have been handed down through the ages, but the majority are unfortunately unreliable and time-consuming to make up. Proprietary stains, however, can be relied upon and are available in two types – water and spirit stain – which are both equally effective for carved work. The water stain does tend to lift the grain, necessitating further light sanding down which, unless great care is taken, can take the stain off edges, thus revealing the lighter wood beneath. In general, spirit stain, which also dries more quickly, is preferable.

CLOTHES DYES

Brightly-coloured carvings are generally unacceptable except in the case of painted ships' figureheads or fairground organs, for example. Clothes dyes, however, can be used to lightly stain wood to produce a flesh tone on a face or perhaps to darken the recesses of the folds in a gown to emphasise the depth. Oil paints can also be used to give a similar effect by painting on sparingly and wiping off immediately with a cloth. The little paint that remains in the grain will provide the tint without concealing the figuring of the wood.

OILED WOOD

Wood that is to be used to contain food needs repeated applications of an edible oil such as olive oil, as this is the only finish that will not impart an unpleasant flavour to food. It will also emphasise the grain and give a nice soft lustre. Where wooden dishes are used to contain greasy foods such as crisps, or fruit containing staining juices, polyurethane varnish is impervious to both and can be easily renewed if damaged.

Linseed and teak oil produce a very attractive soft lustre after repeated applications and then buffing up with a soft cloth. They do, however, darken the wood considerably and it takes a long time to achieve satisfactory results. There are now several oils on the market (for example, Rustin's Danish oil) which achieve similar results and which dry and can be buffed up within a few hours. They also offer a measure of protection for wood which is to be exposed outside. With all oiled finishes great care must be taken to get the wood absolutely smooth before applying as it will penetrate more deeply into the slightly roughened surfaces, so darkening them more than the surrounding wood and forming an ugly dark patch.

FUMING

Fuming is the process by which wood is exposed to the fumes of ammonia causing it to darken from a light creamy colour through to almost black. It has an advantage over staining in that it penetrates more deeply and produces a more even spread of colour. Medieval carvers, who were unable to obtain ammonia, of course, would often store their oak and chestnut boards in the stable above the horses. The ammonia fumes from the horses' urine would slowly turn the boards to a pleasing shade of brown.

Suitable woods for fuming are oak or chestnut but some other woods are also affected although the effect is not always good, so a test piece should be tried first. Fuming is carried out by placing the wood, supported either by drawing pins or suspended from a nail to allow the fumes to circulate round it, in a sealed box containing a wide-necked container such as a saucer. Ensure that the container is not placed too close to the wood or a dark patch will result. It is an advantage if the box has a transparent front of glass or plastic to enable the progress of the colour to be observed. The darkening process can be stopped at any time by simply removing the wood from the fumes. Sapwood is not affected to the same extent as the heartwood so if an even, overall colour is required, sapwood should be avoided. The heightened difference in colour between the heartwood and the sapwood, however, can be most attractive. It is sometimes possible to use the effect to illustrate clouds, for example, in a relief.

BURNING

A pleasant dark brown finish can be obtained by burning the surface of the wood with a clean flame such that from a butane torch. It must be carried out with restraint, of course. The woods treated are soft pines which have a marked grain. The soft early summer wood is more affected than the harder late summer growth, so emphasising the grain characteristics. It also enhances the wood texture once the loose burnt material has been wire brushed away. Finishes such as varnishing and waxing can be used over the burnt areas to improve their appearance further.

BLEACH

Household bleach or oxalic acid may be used to whiten wood or to remove an unpleasant dark spot. The oxalic acid is neutralised afterwards with a strong solution of borax. Both methods are not particularly effective and can leave an unpleasant yellow colour behind. It is suggested that where possible both methods should be avoided.

VARNISH STAIN

Varnish which already contains stain can be a useful way of quickly staining and finishing floorboards, for example, but it has little or no place on carved work where its effects are unreliable.

WOOD HARDENER

It is sometimes desirable to use wood which contains a certain amount of rot. You might come across this when making abstracts from wood that has rotted away in the forest and has been formed by the action of sun, wind and rain into interesting shapes, or wood picked up on the sea-shore which has been moulded by the action of the waves. A wood hardener, of which there are now several on the market (normally used to restore wooden window frames), will render the wood to a stone-like hardness when liberally applied. It will, however, darken the wood considerably and will leave behind patches forming a hard glitter where it has failed to penetrate some areas of the wood. The shine can be removed before the hardener has had time to dry by constantly brushing it with an almost dry brush. It is advisable to apply the hardener outside in the air, or at least in a very well-ventilated room, as the fumes are unpleasant.

GILDING

Gilding can be carried out with gold paint or gilding waxes – both are easily obtainable. They look very well when freshly applied but quickly tarnish, particularly when used outside, making the work look shoddy in a short time. Gold leaf, some examples of which have lasted in perfect condition for centuries, is by far the best method of gilding. It is normally applied over *gesso* which was once made up from parchment cuttings boiled in water but which is now commercially available. The whole process of building up the gesso foundation, and laying the gold leaf on the gold size adhesive, calls for great skill and should not be undertaken without expert guidance. The application of small areas of gold leaf, however, is fairly straightforward and can be undertaken by those with little experience.

The areas to be gilded are coated with gold size and allowed to become tacky. Gold leaf transfer, which is gold leaf sandwiched between sheets of tissue paper, is dabbed gently on to the tacky gold size with a wad of cotton wool, the gold leaf remaining in position when the tissue paper is pulled away. Very dark woods may sometimes show through the gold leaf. To prevent this, gold size-based paint should be used as the adhesive.

REPAIRING CARVINGS

If major damage occurs to a work before the carving is complete it is almost always better to destroy the carving immediately, however difficult the decision to do so. However well concealed the damage may be the carver will always know that it exists and will never be satisfied with the work. Any slight damage, however, can often be completely cut away by careful remodelling, but where this is impossible, as in the case of a gouge cut that has penetrated too deeply, the resulting chip can be glued back using 'super glue'. This sets so rapidly that the chip can be held accurately in place by hand, obviating the need for cramps, which are often difficult or impossible to place in position. It may well be found that when the carving is finished and cleaned up, very little of the damage remains, most of it having been cut away during the finishing.

Old carvings, because they are impossible to replace, occasionally need repair, more particularly those with thin vulnerable sections. These should first be thoroughly cleaned by vigorous scrubbing with a paint brush dipped in white spirit. The carving should then be carefully examined for worm holes and signs of rot; any woodworm present can be killed with a proprietary woodworm killer and the holes filled with beeswax which has been stained to the same colour as the wood. Wood that has become spongy due to rot can be hardened with a wood hardener that is normally used to harden rotted window sills. As the hardener tends to darken the wood the whole carving should be treated in order to avoid dark patches.

Any wood that has split away and can be accurately relocated can be glued back into position using a PVA woodworking adhesive. It is held in position while the glue sets with sticky tape.

Great care should be taken to ensure that the glue does not penetrate and set round the area of the damaged wood, otherwise a white stain will result which will only become obvious when the damaged area has been cleaned up and varnished.

Often the surface area of the damaged section is too small to create a good glue bond – for example, the slender legs of a race-horse or a broken antler on a deer. In this case the joint should be pinned with steel pins; panel pins with the heads removed with side cutting pliers are ideal. The difficulty here is to drill the hole for the pin in such a position that when the damaged sections are pushed together with the pin in position they mate up accurately. This can be achieved by drilling a hole in the end of one of the damaged sections of leg and inserting a panel pin to such a depth that only the tip of the point is protruding. This point will mark the position of the other hole when the damaged sections of leg are properly located and pushed together. The panel pin is then removed, the other section of broken leg drilled in the marked position and a panel pin of sufficient length to join the two sections together inserted. The hole drilled for the panel pin should be of a slightly smaller diameter than the pin itself. This will ensure that the joint remains firmly in position while the adhesive sets.

The adhesive used for this very vulnerable type of repair should be one that generates maximum strength, will not rust the steel pin, and whose glue line will not be too obvious. A resin glue such as Cascamite would be ideal.

6 Method and Design

The ability to carve wood requires little strength and is fairly easily mastered by everyone. Depicting the original idea in wood, however, is much more difficult, with the inflexibility of the medium adding to the problem – once wood is removed it cannot be replaced. A few chalk marks on a block of wood were all that was required by the great medieval carvers. For the less experienced, however, a disciplined method of carving eventually leads to a bolder approach and greater freedom of expression than the tentative nibbling away at a block of wood which usually leads to a lifeless carving. The method described here, and used for all the pages of designs is called *blocking in*. It is carried out in three separate stages: blocking in, bosting in, and the carving of detail. The three stages merge into one another and as experience is gained can almost be eliminated, although even for the very experienced it will be found to be of value.

BLOCKING IN

An accurate, drawn to size line drawing which does not show perspective is required for the blocking in. It is used as a template once the outline has been cut out, by placing it on the side of the cleaned-up block of wood. The outline is then drawn round with a soft pencil, 2B being about right for wood. The wood is removed from outside the lines, either with a bandsaw, if you are lucky enough to own one, or by sawing down to the outline radially at close intervals with a handsaw and then splitting the wood away along the grain with a large bosting in gouge, say a 5/8in (15mm) No. 7 and a mallet. Interior wood, between the legs of an animal, for example, which cannot be sawn out with the bandsaw, can be removed either with the bosting in gouge or a jigsaw after first drilling down into the wood to take the jigsaw blade. Professional-type jigsaws which are needed for this work normally cut down to a depth of about 2 1/2in (64mm) thus enabling a 5in (127mm) block to be tackled when approached from each side. The outside outline can also be cut in this manner with the jigsaw if a bandsaw is not available. This is much quicker than the gouge and mallet and saves time because you will not need to clean up the ragged outline with a round surform file. Up to this stage the carver has been working down to an accurate outline, so all the work of removing the wood has been done confidently and quickly in the knowledge that, provided the outline has not been cut into, only the waste wood has been removed. The clear-cut outline that is left will enable the carver to identify important points of the carving from which further marking out can now be aligned.

All this may seem too obvious. What

isn't quite so obvious is the fact that top, front and back views can now be drawn on the block, and again the wood can be confidently and accurately removed down to the outlines. In this case the outlines have to be drawn on by hand without the assistance of a template as the wood is now irregularly shaped, the side view having already been cut out. It is a simple matter, though, to draw the outlines a little oversize to allow for the final shape to be refined later. Once the top, front, side, and back views have been blocked in it will be possible to deal with other parts of the carving in the same way – for example, a face or a hand can be blocked in. It is not until every possible part of the carving has been blocked in that the second phase, the bosting in, commences. The aim at the end of the blocking in phase is for the carving, when viewed from all directions, to have flat sides and square edges with no rounding of edges or shaping.

THE BOSTING IN

In this phase the actual shaping takes place and the carving comes to life. It is of the greatest importance now that the carver either has a clear idea of what the finished work will look like or has available photographs or drawings of the subject. These must be consulted very frequently throughout the carving as it will come as a surprise to the inexperienced carver just how little we know even of everyday shapes that surround us, and how intense the study has to be in order to get a shape right. During the blocking in phase the wood has been removed confidently and

quickly and clear-cut outlines have been left to enable the carver to see what has been achieved, and the next step forward. Once the bosting in is commenced, however, outlines and marks disappear and the work tends to become untidy and confused. It is at this point that despair usually sets in and, although sufficient wood is left, it is difficult to see from where it should be next removed. This does become obvious, however, if the whole work is kept cleaned up with a round surform. Once this has been done other places then show themselves and in a little while the way forward is clear again. During this phase no attempt should be made to carve in any of the detail.

THE CARVING OF DETAIL

It is during this phase that the detail is carved in, such as hair, muscle, eyes, chip-carved decoration on a gown or horse's harness, and so on. It might be thought that extra wood has to be left to allow for the carving of muscle and hair but this is rarely true as if the original outlines have been drawn accurately they will already have made allowance for this.

DESIGN

The template used for the blocking in decides the shape of the finished carving and no major change can be made once the shape has been cut out. It is obviously of the utmost importance that this template is accurate, so a great deal of work and research needs to be done before it is drawn out.

Although early carvings are a great source of pleasure and satisfaction it will soon be found that it is insufficient merely to depict the likeness of an animal, for example. Something about the projected carving must instil anticipation and excitement in the carver. A suitable project should be researched and considered at length until the moment comes when just the right pose or shape comes into mind. It is then difficult to wait for the moment when the carving can be started. It is this excitement and anticipation that will eventually bring the work to life. For this reason only one work should be undertaken at any one time, otherwise the initial inspiration will be lost and the work will become dull and lifeless.

The ability to draw is a valuable asset to the carver, enabling ideas to be set down and considered at leisure, and where necessary to show a client a prospective work. Drawing, however, is not essential as photographs and pictures can be copied. Indeed, a great deal of good carving is carried out successfully in this way and it will be found that the need to alter and modify pictures to make them suitable for woodcarving will develop drawing skills leading to the eventual ability to draw out and design one's own templates. Every opportunity should be taken, though, to practise sketching, however awful the results may seem at first.

Pictures and photographs which would make an attractive carving are rarely the right size to fit the available wood. They show perspective and the outlines usually need to be much more solid to make them suitable for wood.

The picture can be scaled up or down using a grid which is drawn on the picture and an appropriately-sized grid drawn on the paper. It is then a simple matter to scale the drawing up or down by filling in the outlines in the squares. The ragged outline that results can then be cleaned up and at the same time corrections made for the distortions caused by perspective. For example, the far legs of a horse will be shown further off the ground than the near legs in the picture, or the far ear will be smaller than the near ear if the head is turned, which will obviously need correcting. The outlines, too, are rarely solid enough for wood and should generally be made thicker. If this is overdone it can easily be corrected later during the carving.

An alternative method of scaling up or down is by using an epidiascope; an inexpensive one is quite satisfactory for this purpose. The image is thrown on to a sheet of paper and adjusted to a size that will fit the available stock. Then the outlines and any necessary detail are simply filled in, corrected for perspective and solidity as before. The epidiascope is particularly useful when using your own photographs, as views of the subject can be taken which would not normally be available. For example, the back view of a horse may be inelegant but it is essential for the successful carving. This also leads to much greater freedom of choice.

Once the drawing has been roughed out in this way the base must be considered. Its shape and finish should be designed to balance and complement the carving. It is often difficult to decide on a suitable shape and size but this can be made easier by cutting out the shape of the carving from light card or paper, leaving a large piece in the base position. The paper is then folded up into different shapes and viewed with the eyes half closed. At the same time an attempt should be made to visualise the width of the base as it cannot be seen in the side view. It will often be found that a length of base that looks right from the side will present too large a bare area when viewed from the more normal position of the top. The type of base is also important; the ornate polished base required to complement the superb elegance of the race-horse is probably quite unsuitable for the massive strength and beauty of the Shire.

Holding the carving as work proceeds should also be considered as it is sometimes possible to leave a block of wood on the base to be removed when the carving is complete. Alternatively, the base itself may be used to hold the work as it is left until last before being carved.

CLAY MODELS

Although the template is ideal for straightforward carvings, more complex work requires a clay model to be made up in order to check the balance of the work in the round and to ensure that all angles are correct. It is a great temptation in a line drawing to have feet pointing straight ahead instead of being splayed out at an angle or to turn a head without angling it over slightly. Points like these quickly become obvious in the clay model. Modelling clay is readily available quite cheaply and even when it has been used and dried out it can be reconstituted with water and kept in good condition in a sealed plastic bag which has had a damp rag enclosed with it. Small carvings can be success-

fully modelled in clay without needing support. For larger models, however, it is necessary to make up an armature from available bits such as dowelling, lengths of rod, old chicken wire, and so on. A base board is required which is rigid enough to support the armature, and pieces of rod are stuck into holes drilled in the base board. Crumpled chicken wire can be wound round these and glued in position with epoxy resin glue.

It is a great help to have the clay in a good, workable condition before attempting to model with it. A great deal of kneading is required, but when the right consistency is achieved it will become obvious – the clay will no longer stick to the fingers yet it will not be so dry that it will crumble in the hand.

Sculptors' modelling tools are available at little cost from all art shops but it will be found that the fingers and perhaps the back of a spoon or similar instrument will be all the tools required.

The model should be retained throughout the carving as it is often valuable to be able to refer to it, to take measurements with dividers or to try out ideas as the work proceeds, such as different hair arrangements or decorative finishes. The clay will quickly dry and crumble away from the armature unless it is kept damp. An occasional spray of water from a house-plant spray will keep it moist whilst it is uncovered and covering it with a plastic bag with damp rags in it will keep it in good condition when stored.

The clay model may be all that is required for the more advanced carver to work from but it is more usual to draw out the line drawing that will form the template with the knowledge gained from the modelling as well. It may seem an obvious point to make but the template must fit the stock available. Often shakes or knots in the wood are overlooked because it has been insufficiently cleaned up and the drawing then has to be redrawn or modified to allow for these.

The design must be right for the wood. It must make use of all its lovely characteristics – its strength, warmth, grain, tactility, colour, solidity, and permanence. Rightness for wood is difficult to define but a careful study of old carvings, particularly church carvings, will lead to an understanding of this. Points to be avoided are undue fussiness and designs that use an inordinate amount of expensive wood. The outstretched arm of a figure could double the amount of wood required, and it would also be vulnerable to damage. The wood that is available must also be considered. It would be quite wrong to attempt to carve fine detail into an open-grained wood such as oak or to carve the slender legs of a race-horse from a light mahogany such as utile. Grain can also be used not only as a point of great beauty in itself but to depict, say, clouds in a relief or the movement of sea. Even knots or discol-

oration caused by water staining can sometimes be made use of by careful study of the wood during the design stage.

There are no rules or short cuts – only the study of the work of other people and the carver's own love and understanding of wood will lead to good design. A carving that has been designed to make best use of the solidity and strength of wood could well last for centuries, in many cases providing the continuity and interest seen in fine pieces of furniture. It adds considerably to the interest of the work if the carver's mark and date are carved on it somewhere. The mark is usually a monogram made up of the carver's initials – a design that belongs uniquely to the carver, which looks attractive and which is straightforward to carve is well worth taking some time over.

An additional interest is to take a series of photographs of each stage of the carving which would perhaps include shots of the carver and his family. These can be made up into an album with a diary noting the progress of the work, the type of wood used and where it was obtained. This will not only add greatly to the interest of the work but also add to its value if it is ever considered for sale.

7 Types of Carving

Woodcarving can be divided into four groups: chip carving, whittling, relief, and work in the round or sculpture in wood. The tools used in each group can differ and even the gouge bevels can be made more acute or obtuse to suit the type of work in hand. It is as well, therefore, to consider the type of carving to be carried out before making a choice of tools, although the first four gouges shown in the suggested list in Chapter 1 are good general-purpose gouges and will be of use whatever type of carving is undertaken.

WHITTLING

Whittling is the earliest known and simplest form of carving. Softwoods are generally used and the availability of these and the fact that only a knife is required make whittling a very popular pastime, particularly in the United States where quite remarkable work is achieved with the knife alone. It does have severe limitations, though, and cannot be compared with carving with gouges.

CHIP CARVING

Chip carving is a simple but effective method of decorating a plain wooden surface. It needs to be used with restraint but viewed in a good light that shows up the shadows it can be very effective.

A sharp pointed knife is the only tool required, although more accuracy and cleaner cutting can be achieved with a set of chip carving knives. Suitably-shaped gouges can also be used.

The method of carving is simplicity itself. Three angled cuts are made in the surface of the wood in such a way that a clean triangular chip comes away leaving a triangular-shaped depression behind. Sometimes, to heighten the effect, a dark-stained white wood is used, the triangular depression showing up white against the dark background. The chip can also be cut out with a small fluter gouge by first stabbing down vertically and then cutting along horizontally until the chip comes away cleanly.

RELIEF CARVING

Relief carving ranges from shallow incised work to work that is almost in the round, where the main elements of the design are nearly severed from the background. The Italian carvers were able to achieve a quite remarkable feeling of depth in very shallow reliefs and this is the effect to aim for in this type of carving. It is more difficult than it appears at first, and a good deal of thought has to be given to the various levels of the carving before work commences. It is the only form of carving in which perspective has to be taken into account, but it has the advantage that it can be carried out on small flat pieces of readily-available stock.

WORK IN THE ROUND

Work in the round, or sculpture in wood, allows the carver free imaginative rein, subject only to the limitations of the medium. Thin easily-broken sections, for example, and designs that use an inordinate amount of expensive wood, are best avoided. After that, the only limiting factors are the imagination and expertise of the carver. It is the most exciting and rewarding form of carving, its main difficulty being the comparatively large pieces of stock required and the need, unlike most other art forms, to see the work in three dimensions.

8 Inlay

The technique of inlaying materials into wood is almost as old as woodcarving itself. Used with good taste and restraint inlay can do much to enhance a carving and where necessary emphasise important points which might otherwise be overwhelmed by grain or colour. Although inlay into furniture, with its flat surfaces and straight edges available as a guide, is well documented it is surprising how little information there is for the woodcarver who has irregularly-shaped surfaces to contend with. It will be found that methods and techniques have to be worked out by the individual carver by experiment. The following methods and tips have been successfully used by myself over the years but I am sure that there are many more tricks possible.

MATERIALS FOR INLAY

The types or combinations of materials that can be used for inlay are almost endless. The main consideration in making a choice is to find a harmonious colour which will also provide sufficient contrast. Wood alone is our particular medium, of course, but other possibilities are bone, ivory, silver, brass, copper and stone.

Bone

Bone is a surprisingly hard substance and, as with metals, it is an advantage to have power and metal-working tools when using it. Unlike most inlays it requires some initial preparation. Large marrow bones should be obtained and the end knuckles removed, the remainder being sawn into about 3in (76mm) lengths. The marrow is removed, preferably by the dog, and the bones boiled in water to which a little household bleach has been added. When all the fat and gristle have been boiled away the bones are ready for use. If it is intended to store them for any length of time it is an advantage to leave them in a sunny spot such as the greenhouse, as the sun's ultraviolet light will continue to bleach them to a startling white. Although difficult to work, bone makes first-class inlay as it is quite stable and provides a good sharp contrast with the wood (which it will almost certainly outlast).

Ivory

Ivory is very similar to bone to work and can be bleached by the sun in the same way. It does, however, tend to yellow with time and it is as well to remember that some of the methods of obtaining it involve a great deal of cruelty. This puts me very much against its use.

Silver

Silver is now very expensive although the small amount usually required will not add a prohibitive cost to the work, and its colour shows up very well, particularly against the darker woods. It is easy to obtain as most jewellers stock it in a variety of forms. The most popular is wire which is very simple to inlay. It is also obtainable in strips which have a pierced pattern stamped through them, and there are also sheets of varying thicknesses which are easily cut and shaped with tinsnips. Silver, like copper or brass, requires a clear varnish or lacquer coating to prevent it tarnishing. This is normally done when the wood is finished, the wax applied later also helping to polish and preserve it.

Stone

In most forms stone is not entirely suitable for inlay. Small stones found on the beach and polished in a polishing machine, however, can be used to good effect in, say, the crown of a carved princess or to decorate a harness. There are many applications that will add to the beauty and complement the carving, and the need to study various types of suitable stone opens up a new world of interest. It is also great fun for the whole family to search for, and find, beautifully-coloured stones on the beach.

Woods for Inlay

The most suitable woods for inlay are straight-grained dense hardwoods. Holly is the best of the native hardwoods as it is easy to obtain in the small quantities required and is very white. It does contain brown stripes but these are easily avoided. For those intending to inlay at some future date it is a good idea to obtain a few small branches – there are nearly always a few misshapen ones which can be removed without harming the tree. They should be sawn into about 1/2in (12mm) wide straight strips after the bark has been removed, and left to dry out in the workshop. Any checks or curling can then be avoided when the inlay wood is required.

There are many other suitable English hardwoods such as hawthorn, which is very hard and white, lime (linden), which is a creamy-white, or sycamore, a whitish colour. It is possible to keep a small store to hand of suitable colours and textures, particularly box, which is ideal from every point of view – its soft creamy-yellow colour rarely clashes with other coloured woods.

Of the darker woods ebony is the most suitable, but it is almost impossible to obtain in anything other than very thin strips which, although helpful, do not cover the range required. Most mahoganys inlay well but the red colouring does not always harmonise with the colour of the carving. Where it does fit in it can be very effective indeed and is well worth considering. If it is decided that a very dark wood is essential and ebony is not available, chestnut could be considered as a last resort. It could be inlaid in its natural colour and then fumed to the depth of colour required in a fuming cabinet. The wood of the carving would need to be impervious to ammonia fumes and only heartwood of the chestnut would be suitable as the sapwood is not affected. Great care has to be taken to ensure that no adhesive is left in the grain as this would prevent the penetration of the fumes, resulting in light-coloured spots.

INLAY TECHNIQUES

Dowelling

Probably the simplest form of inlaying is by use of the dowel. A hole is drilled in the wood and a dowel, with a touch of adhesive on the end, is tapped in. The dowel is sawn off with a junior hacksaw blade just proud of the wood and then filed flush with the surface. Any attempt to sand it flush would result in two different levels being formed due to the difference in hardness between the two woods. It is tempting to drill the hole a smaller size in order to ensure a tight fit but this only results in the wood being compressed round the perimeter of the hole leaving an irregularly-shaped recess at this point. An alternative to filing the dowel flush is to leave it proud, rounding off the protruding wood into the shape of a dome. This will form an attractive rosette when intersected by two V cuts made with a triangular file at right angles to one another. The shaped dome can be filed with a fine file of course but if there are a lot to do, a perfect dome can be quickly formed by drilling a shallow spherical hole in a length of suitably-sized rod and making a hacksaw cut across it to form a cutting edge. When this is rotated over the protruding dowel in a hand brace a dome will be quickly and accurately formed. If required it can be drilled down low enough to enable the end of the rod to form a narrow anulus round the dome which makes an additional feature.

Dowels can be made up by using a dowel plate. This is a piece of mild steel plate which has a series of holes, progressively increasing in size, drilled in it. A hacksaw cut from the edge of the plate into each hole provides a cutting edge. A square length of wood, about 2in (51mm) long with the sides about the width of the diameter of the dowel and with the edges roughly filed off, is driven down through the appropriate hole in the dowel plate by means of a slowly turned hand brace. This will produce a clean accurate dowel. The more normal method of tapping the squared wood through the dowel plate with a hammer does not produce an accurate enough dowel for our purpose. In the case of bone or ivory the speed of a power drill is necessary to drive the square dowel through the plate. In this case a mask and goggles are essential for safety.

A variation on the plain circle of inlay that is left in the wood is to drill out the centre of the inlay and insert a dowel that has been made up from the same wood as the carving. When this is filed flush the finished result looks like an inlaid ring. So that the side grain rather than the end grain of the dowel is visible, a plug of wood can be cut by using a short length of tube that has had a bevel filed on the end to make a cutting edge. When turned slowly in a hand brace this will cut into the surface of a piece of wood and, when deep enough, the plug will snap off as the tube is angled over. The plug can then be pushed out of the tube and inserted in the drilled hole. If care is taken to line up the grain the plug will be impossible to detect. The plug can also be inserted off-centre so forming a crescent shape. In this case, however, it is important that the drill point is kept within the perimeter of the inserted inlay, otherwise the difference in the hardness of the dowel and the surface wood will cause the drill to run off.

Occasionally it is desirable to have an oval inlay as, for example, in the centre of a horse's nose band. This can still be done using the round dowel by drilling into the wood at a sharp angle leaving an oval shape once the dowel has been inserted and filed flush. The drilling of the hole must be done with great care. The drill should be perfectly sharp and the wood centre punched before starting, otherwise the drill will tend to run off.

Inlaying Shaped Inlay

Inlaying dowelling and the variations that are possible is a simple straightforward job. The inlaying of flat-shaped pieces of inlay, particularly on rounded or convex surfaces, is much more difficult.

The thickness of the inlay wood required will vary with the type of surface into which it is to be inserted. A rounded or convex surface requires a greater thickness than a flat one in general although 1/8in (3mm) is about right. Many marquetry veneers are about this thickness and represent a very convenient method of obtaining suitable wood. They also save the very accurate cutting required when they are sawn from a rough bough.

Once the inlay shape has been decided on, a paper template should be produced and stuck temporarily in position by being dampened. Once it has been satisfactorily checked for accuracy it can be

glued to the inlay wood with a contact adhesive which can easily be removed later before it dries. The paper should be dark-coloured for light woods and white for dark woods. This makes it very much easier to follow the outline accurately when it is being fretted out.

If, as is usual, the piece of inlay is very small, it is better to fret it out from a large piece of wood, which can be clamped or held by hand. If sufficient wood is not available the inlay wood can be glued to a piece of thin but larger wood using a contact adhesive which will hold it sufficiently firmly, but which can be easily removed before it has completely dried after fretting out.

Fretsaws

Fretsawing can be carried out with either a hand saw or a power-driven saw. The hand saw is quite adequate but it is difficult to keep it exactly upright, particularly when fretting complex shapes, and this can result in an unsightly gap around the inlay. Power-driven saws are available in three main types. The vibrating saw, which oscillates at mains frequency, does not live up to the claims made for it and, although useful for very thin inlay, it is useless for bone or ivory. The reciprocating fretsaw is ideal as the blade speed is much lower, but it is very expensive. The relatively small amount of use it has from the carver rarely justifies the expense. Treadle-driven fretsaws are probably the best of the three types, the blade speed being easily adjusted. When, as frequently happens, the blade jams, it can immediately be stopped.

For those carvers contemplating a fair

amount of inlay it is possible to make up a foot-operated fretsaw quite easily from the bits box which would be suitable for small inlays. The method of construction will be discussed at the end of this chapter.

Once the inlay is fretted out it needs to be held firmly in the required position so that its recess can be accurately marked out. Again the contact adhesive is used, the inlay being removed before it has had time to set. Where the inlay is to be put into a concave or convex surface the back of the inlay must be shaped with a file to fit the surface before it is glued into position. In this case the inlay thickness must take account of the shaping. The top surface of the inlay can be left flat to be filed flush later.

The inlay recess is marked out with a sharp, pointed knife following the outline of the inlay, with the knife slightly angled outwards for accuracy. The inlay is then prised off before the adhesive has had time to set and the outline deepened slightly with the point of the knife. Any attempt to force the knife in too deeply will result in a wide cut and a gap round the finished inlay. Wood between the lines can be removed with a small flattish gouge, say a 1/8in (3mm) No. 3, and the process repeated until the required depth is reached. The inlay, of approximately 1/8in (3mm), when tapped gently into the recess, should fit snugly and stand a little proud. It is not necessary for the bottom of the recess to match the bottom of the inlay accurately as a gap-filling epoxy resin adhesive is used to glue it in position. In fact a slight roughness at the bottom of the recess assists in a

good glue bond. Once the adhesive has set the inlay can be filed flush using a fine file or, as is sometimes required, left a little proud, the top surface being shaped to match the surface of the carving. Once the adhesive has set and the inlay has been filed flush it should be dampened to make the wood swell, thus filling any possible tiny gaps.

The inlay itself can also be drilled and inlaid as suggested for the dowelling, but this is not for the inexperienced.

Although it is neither carving nor inlay, it is sometimes possible for small decorative features to be added to a carving, making use of the inlay wood and of the tools that have been used for inlay. For example, the plumes on the top of a circus horse's head harness can be formed from a piece of dowel made in the dowel plate and turned in the chuck of a power drill. It is shaped by files and strips of sandpaper and then glued into a hole drilled in the head harness. Buckles on harness straps can be fretted out and filed up into decorative shapes. With a little thought the possibilities are endless, with the only restraint being the need both for good taste and not to overwhelm or detract from the carving.

The Foot-Operated Fretsaw (Operation)

Heath Robinson could never have considered anything as bizarre as this and yet it is simply made and works satisfactorily for the very small pieces of inlay used. The accompanying photographs (Figs 16 and 17) make the construction self-explanatory.

The body of the saw in the photograph was made from a solid block of wood

Fig 16 Foot-operated fretsaw, for use when very low speeds are required, such as when sawing small pieces of hard inlay out of bone.

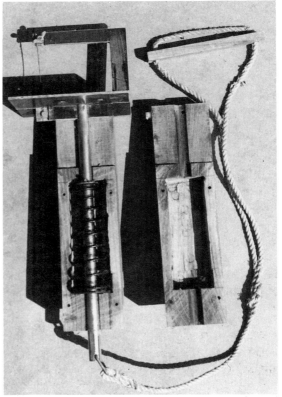

Fig 17 Foot-operated fretsaw sectioned to show the construction.

simply because a rather nice piece of elm happened to be available. It could be just as easily made up from 1/2in (12mm) planks with the joints dowelled and glued together. The block was sawn in half along its length and each half routed out to form a cavity large enough to take a suitably-sized spring, in this case from an old foot pump. The groove in which the tube slides was also routed out in each half and the top recessed to allow the frame to move up and down freely with no undue play, so

locating the frame fore and aft. The frame and table were made up from two sheets of Paxolin glued together with epoxy resin to give rigidity. The frame was then fitted into a slot cut in the top of the tube and riveted in position. The blade was secured to the frame by a bolt wing nut and washer on the top and bottom arms.

The tube was drilled through with a small drill at the top of the spring position and a small pin was tapped through the hole with a washer placed underneath. The spring is compressed when the tube is pulled down and will extend, so pushing up the tube and frame, when released.

A length of strong cord is attached to the bottom of the tube and passed through two holes drilled in a piece of wood to form a foot rest, the cord being of sufficient length almost to touch the floor when extended. To operate the saw, the body of the saw is placed in a vice and the frame moved up and down with the foot. Held like this the saw table is just at a convenient height from which to view the work as it is being sawn.

9 Ideas for Carvings

When considering the vast range of possible subjects open to the woodcarver it is surprising how difficult it is to decide what to carve next. There always seems to be some reason why a particular project is unsuitable – either the available wood is the wrong size, grain, colour, texture or perhaps the vast range of possibilities is off-putting. Whatever the reason, getting started is one of the carver's major hurdles.

Although it is tempting to start on a large complex work in the round it is far better to lead up to the more difficult work in gradual stages, starting with the small items that can be so decorative and useful around the house.

Bowls

One might think that bowls are more the province of the turner as it is possible to turn and finish a bowl so much more easily and quickly than to carve it. The turner, however, is limited to turning round bowls which quickly become dull, while the carver can carve any shape that he cares to imagine and, when required, decorate it with carving. Any hardwood would be suitable, although for bowls used to contain food an aromatic wood should be avoided.

Trays

Trays used to hold small items, one of which is described in the chapter on designs, are not only straightforward to carve and attractive but also functional. I saw a tray similar to the one illustrated being carved in Honolulu over thirty years ago. The little tray that I made as a result has served as a pen and pencil holder in my writing bureau ever since.

Bread Boards

Bread boards normally have a bevel about 1 1/2in (38mm) wide around the circumference to give clearance for the cutting edge of the bread knife. This bevel is an ideal surface on which to carve ears of wheat, for example, an appropriate and easy decoration.

Bookends

Bookends carved from a solid block seem to be right for wood, although an acceptable alternative is to carve a relief or an incised design on a piece of hardwood about 1in (25mm) thick and to screw a piece of metal sheet, preferably brass, on the bottom to form a right angle. The wood is kept upright when books are placed on the metal sheet. Bookends carved from a solid block offer much more scope. Carved animals' heads, particularly if they happen to be the heads of dearly-loved pets, make wonderful presents and will bring back fond memories long after the pet has gone.

Fig 18 Hector bookend – a practical way of remembering a dearly-loved pet.

The bookend carving of Hector (Fig 18), which is a little more advanced and requires the skills of the more experienced carver, was intended to depict not only the likeness of the old dog but to show a particular characteristic, in this case his habit of flopping back against a table or chair-leg. This is an endearing pose, and very indicative of the dog's character. Sadly he is no longer with us, but the bookend will provide a lasting and pleasant memory for his master.

Newel Posts

Newel posts when carved can transform a quite ordinary staircase, especially if they are finished off with a nicely carved acorn on the top. The four sides lend themselves ideally to depicting the four seasons with daffodils for spring, wheat ears for summer, oak for autumn, and holly for winter. Carving a newel post in situ would be very difficult but 3/4in (19mm) planks carved and secured to the four sides would get over this problem and improve the appearance of the post by making it look more substantial.

Fireplace Surrounds

Fireplace surrounds can be dealt with in the same way. The glow from a warm fire looks very well indeed when it lights up the carved surfaces.

Nameboards

A well-designed and carved nameboard for the house will add considerably to its appearance, especially if it includes in its design an interest of the owner, such as a mermaid for a mariner or dog's head for a dog lover. Hailboards for the sterns of boats lend themselves particularly well to carved decoration and are very saleable items for the proud boat owner.

Love Spoons

Love spoons are usually whittled with a knife and as such are not regarded as true carving. Still, they are good fun to whittle and can get surprisingly complicated, with the inclusion of chains carved from the solid wood or balls in a cage forming part of the handle.

Butter Moulds

Butter or pastry moulds can be a useful

item for those who enjoy cooking. They need to be carved in a wood that will take fine details such as lime (linden). They are quite difficult to follow as they are being carved because the work is inset instead of in relief. Damp bread pressed into the mould will take its shape and make it easier to follow. This work is know as *intaglio,* and is the opposite of relief.

Walking Stick Handles

Walking stick handles have been carved for centuries and some very fine examples exist today. Usually they are whittled instead of carved, but the possibilities they present are endless.

Spinning Chairs

Spinning chairs look extremely well when carved and polished with a nice glowing wax polish, and make a useful additional chair when one is required. The back can be quite deeply carved in relief though it is usual only to incise any decorative carving on the seat, otherwise one tends to become embossed!

A spinning chair project which might be considered is one similar to that carried out by a student of mine. Her husband constructed the chair, the legs were turned by her daughter, my student did the carving and their niece designed a monogram consisting of their four initials which was then carved in the middle of the chair back. It looked extremely good when finished and is certainly destined to become a family heirloom with an interesting history.

Shelf Brackets

A shelf bracket seems at first a very ordinary subject for the woodcarver and yet a good, solid, crisply-carved bracket in an interesting theme can transform a whole room. So many fine examples abound that it is not worth listing all the various possibilities, except perhaps to say that pierced carvings might be considered as a variation on the more usual solid bracket.

Abstracts

Abstracts designed with a particular block of wood in mind can do so much to enhance the natural beauty of the grain and can sometimes even make use of faults in the wood such as checks and loose knots. It is important that in any design the mass of the carving must be balanced when viewed from any direction and that it complements and expresses the inherent solidity of wood. It is often difficult to know where to start when designing an abstract. A clay model is a great help as it can be quickly formed and altered at will. Shadows cast against a piece of white paper will often suggest a suitable design or you can just cut into a block of wood and see what happens. I have seen some very good results achieved like that, but in general (as with all carving) it is better to start off with a very clear-cut idea of what the end result will eventually look like.

Rotted tree branches and roots found in woods and forests which have been shaped by the action of wind, sun, and rain over the centuries can make ideal abstracts, taking shapes impossible for the human brain to imagine or the

Fig 19 What could be done with a piece of rotting Turkey oak . . . ?

human hand to fashion. After cleaning and being hardened with a wood hardener they can be mounted, perhaps on a carved or polished base. It may be that a shape in the wood will suggest an idea to you which can be carved leaving the rest of the wood in its natural condition (Figs 19 and 20). Covered in mud and moss the useful pieces are difficult to recognise in the forest, and on many occasions I have with great difficulty carried a piece home only to find it unsuitable when cleaned up. When a suitable piece is found, however, it makes it all worth while. In any case it is great fun for the whole family to find and carry home these treasures, and as I have found to my cost they are very attractive to those who like flower arranging.

It might be imagined that driftwood would be similar in appearance to forest wood, but the action of sand and water on the wood is quite different although the final result can be just as beautiful and interesting. The sand that becomes ingrained in the wood does tend to take the edge off tools so that where possible the carving of driftwood should be avoided.

Ships' Figureheads

The carving of the great ships'

Fig 20 . . . Well, how about this!

figureheads is a specialised form of carving. Their sheer bulk puts them beyond the reach of most carvers but there is a steady market for them and the fascinating history and legends that surround figureheads is a worthwhile study in itself. It is said that the old sailors trusted a beautiful woman at the bow to guide them through the stormy night, with her eyes scanning the horizon for danger, never looking up or down; and when the head of a figurehead is turned, it is always to the right or starboard, for the old mariners had the interesting and invaluable theory that a cabin boy didn't become a man until he could spit to windward when rounding Cape Horn

in the face of the dreadful gales blowing offshore. Female figureheads were also expected to be of ample proportions to give some comfort to the stout fellows who were away from home for long periods.

Although many figureheads have now sadly rotted away, some are still preserved and even those that have been destroyed are quite often well documented. Scale models of these are well within the scope of all carvers and are very saleable items, particularly if care is taken to make them as authentic as possible.

Totem Poles

As with ships' figureheads the scope of totem poles makes it difficult to carve them life-size, but again scale models can be carved. The original totem poles represented a form of picture language in which the history of a family or tribe was depicted in carving. The whole thing was surmounted by the totem which was chosen to indicate some desirable characteristic of the family, such as a bear for strength or a fox for cunning. It would be an intriguing and imaginative exercise to design and carve a totem pole based on one's own family history – I can imagine that in some cases the result would be, to say the least, interesting!

For the vast majority of woodcarvers, many of whom take up woodcarving during retirement, the satisfaction of creative work is sufficient reward in itself. There are those, however, who quite properly seek to recover their costs or make a living from woodcarving. This requires a quite different approach, although it is no less interesting. In fact the need to execute a commission in a certain way often leads the craftsman into fields of research and carving that would not otherwise have been considered. For the beginner a start on straightforward work, such as house nameboards or boat hailboards, will help to build up experience and if the work is well designed and executed this will lead to further work. As experience is gained the scope widens to items such as ships' figureheads, fairground organs and church carvings which, because of their age, often require considerable restoration. The skills required for this command a good return. Work should be exhibited at every possible opportunity. Whether it is sold or not is not important – the advertisement is there and your name gets known.

Both teaching and writing can supplement the carver's income and with this in mind it will be of considerable value to keep a diary of work done, and photographs of the stages of each carving, in order to be able to refer to it in later years.

Although few carvers are destined to become rich, the independence and rewards from a creative way of life working in the most beautiful of mediums is more than sufficient recompense.

10 Designs

As can be seen by the accompanying photographs all the following designs were based on actual carvings and the tools that were used for the work are the ones described in the text. For the inexperienced carver who needs to gain dexterity with tools and become familiar with the feel of wood, it would be as well to use the tools suggested and to copy the first few designs as they are shown in the drawings. As experience and confidence are gained it is of the utmost importance that the carver views the designs critically and if necessary changes them to suit his particular taste. Only this individual approach will produce a vital, lively and interesting work.

Any major change in the design must be made to the drawing before the wood is blocked in, although minor alterations can be made as the work progresses. It is always tempting to save time and work by the straightforward copying of designs and pictures, but this must be resisted at all costs. An individual and imaginative approach should be made to every carving. When the carver already possesses a set of carving tools which have become familiar with use it would be far better to use these than those suggested in the text. A sound general rule is to use a much larger gouge than is at first felt necessary.

The approximate relative difficulty of each design is indicated by a scale of numbers ranging from one to five, with the most difficult designs being Scale 5.

THE HAWAIIAN LEAF TRAY (SCALE 1)

The shape of this tray was based on the shape of a Hawaiian leaf. It is not only an attractive shape but has proved for me a most useful one. There are, however, an endless variety of leaf forms which would be just as useful and beautiful in our own countryside, the chestnut or the sycamore being two good examples. It would not be difficult even for the beginner to design a tray based upon a suitable leaf, and then to follow the procedure for carving it as shown in the text. The carver's own design would also help to make the best use of any available wood as it could be made to fit the wood or avoid, or even make use of, checks and grain. The tray illustrated could be altered to suit the carver's preference; for example, the edge could be undulating as in an actual leaf instead of straight, or leaf veins could be incised on the bowl of the tray.

Any wood would be suitable, although a strongly-figured hardwood such as ash would both look and finish very well.

Method of Carving

Produce a template from the drawing and use it to mark out the wood. Cut out the shape with a coping saw, or, if you are lucky enough to possess one, a bandsaw or jigsaw. The hole in the stem can be sawn out with the coping

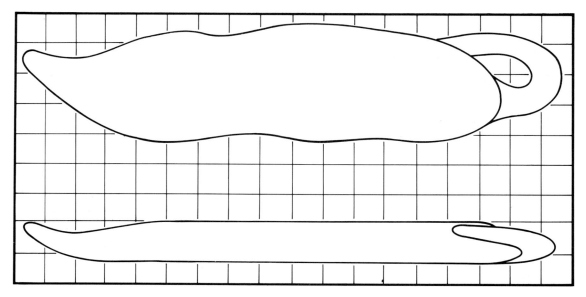

Fig 21 Template for the Hawaiian leaf tray.

saw after first drilling through it to take the saw blade. Glue a block of wood approximately 2 1/2×2 1/2in (62×62mm) to the top and bottom of the tray to enable it to be held safely and securely in the vice (Fig 22).

Mark in the wood to be removed from the tray tip and the stem as shown by the shaded areas in Fig 22. Remove wood from the top and bottom of the tip with a 5/8in (15mm) No.7 and a mallet, smoothing it off with a round or half-round surform. Remove wood from the shaded parts of the stem with a 3/8in (9mm) No.6 after first forming a channel where the stem meets the side of the tray with a 3/8in (9mm) No.10. This will form a stop cut to prevent the 3/8in (9mm) No.6 over-running and digging into the tray side. Clean up the stem with the round surform noting that the surfaces have been kept flat, no attempt having been made at this stage to round them off (Fig 23).

Mark a line round the tray about 1/4in (6mm) down from the top edge and a further line round the bottom, about 3/4in (19mm) in from the side (Fig 23). Round over the bottom edge between these two lines removing the bulk of the wood with the 5/8in (15mm) No.7 and finishing off with the round surform, ensuring that the tip is contoured smoothly into the bottom of the tray. Round over the stem with a 3/8in (9mm) No.6, smoothing it and contouring into the tray side with a medium-cut round rat tail file. Finish the smoothing and contouring with strips of 100 grit sandpaper pulled back and forth with two hands, after first securing sticky tape to the back of the strips to prevent them breaking (Fig 24).

Clean up as much of the bottom of the tray as possible with files and sandpaper before cutting off the top block with the 5/8in (15mm) No.7. The removal of the block will enable the tray to be hollowed out. Mark a line round the top surface of the tray approximately 3/16in (4.5mm) in from the edge and make a series of gouge cuts across

66

Fig 22

Fig 23

Fig 24

Fig 25   The finished Hawaiian leaf tray, ideal for use as a pen and pencil holder.

68

it with the 5/8in (15mm) No.7, allowing the gouge to run out of the wood about 1/2in (12mm) before it reaches the other side in order to prevent the edge splitting away. Make the cuts evenly from one end to the other and then turn the tray round and repeat the process starting now from the other edge. Continue like this until the bottom is approximately 3/8in (9mm) thick. It is important that the cuts are kept as even as possible to save time cleaning up later.

Smoothing the inside of the tray will be quite difficult. First remove all the ridges formed by the 5/8in (15mm) No.7 with a flatter gouge, say a 5/8in (15mm) No.3, then scrape out all the gouge marks left with either a carver's scraper or, perhaps better still, a cabinet scraper which has had radii of different sizes ground on each corner. Another alternative is to use a piece of broken glass, choosing a piece of about the right contour. Finish the inside of the tray by sanding with reducing grades of sandpaper ensuring that the inside of the tip is contoured smoothly into the bowl of the tray (Fig 25).

The top edge of the tray should now be about 3/16in (4.5mm) thick. Round over the outer edge with a flat file until it meets the inner edge, this will give a thin but strong edge which will not be easily damaged. Remove the bottom block by splitting it away with the 5/8in (15mm) No.7 taking great care not to damage the bottom of the tray, and finish cleaning up the whole of the bottom with the scraper files and sandpaper.

Wipe the tray over with a damp rag to raise the grain and when completely dry rub down with flour-grade sandpaper. Rough patches which have been previously missed will now become obvious. These can be scraped out and finished with sandpaper.

Finishing

This type of tray is often used to hold greasy food such as potato crisps or fruit with staining juices. A polyurethane varnish should be used to prevent the wood from becoming soiled; if the harsh glitter of the varnish is found unacceptable it can be gently rubbed down with 0 grade steel wool and then wax polished. Any staining that now occurs can be removed with the 0 grade steel wool dipped in wax polish.

THE PENGUIN (SCALE 1)

Penguins have such an endearing, jolly appearance that it makes them a very attractive subject for the woodcarver and, apart from the slender beak, there are no thin, vulnerable sections which could be easily damaged. This design overcomes the vulnerability of the beak to some extent by arranging it to follow the directions of the grain so avoiding crossgrain at this vulnerable point, and creating a pose that is very characteristic of all penguin species. Both these points are important and among others should always be considered when a carving is being designed. The shape of the base makes it ideal for clamping in the vice, which in this case makes a screwed block of wood on the base unnecessary. Care should be taken, however, to ensure that the wood of the base is not bruised by the vice jaws. A piece of hardboard made to fit over each jaw will prevent this damage. The simple angular shape

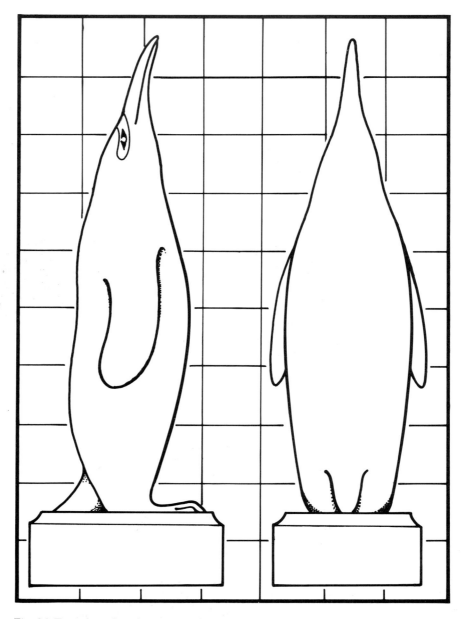

Fig 26 Template for the penguin carving.

of the base contrasts well with the shape of the carving but other alternatives can be considered to make the carving individual; for example, rocks would look well and be appropriate. Any alteration must be considered and the template altered before the work is blocked in.

Blocking In

Produce a template from the side-view drawing and use it to mark out the block of wood. Remove wood from outside the lines with a 5/8in (15mm) No.7 and a mallet. Draw on the two lines marking the top and bottom extremities

of the wings as shown in the shaded area in Fig 27. This will prevent this wood being removed by mistake.

Draw on the back and front views by hand after first drawing in a centre line to assist in keeping both sides equal.

Again mark in the top and bottom extremities of the wings, this time on the back view and remove wood from outside the lines with the 5/8in (15mm) No.7. Clean up the whole work with a round surform keeping all surfaces flat and making no attempt to round off or shape the carving (Fig 28).

Mark in the side view of the bottom of the rear of the legs and remove wood

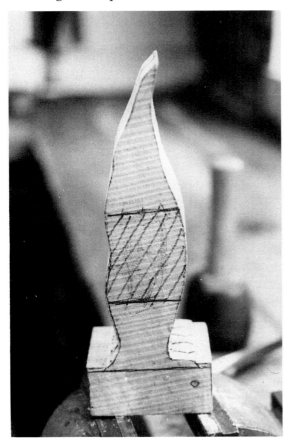

Fig 27

Fig 28

71

down as far as the tail with a 3/8in (9mm) No.6, removing the ridges left by the gouge with a 3/8in (9mm) No.3.

Make up a template of the wing and use it to mark out the wing positions on each side of the body. Define the shape of the wings with a 1/4in (6mm) No.9 and remove the waste wood down as far as the body with the 3/8in (9mm) No.6. The wings should now be standing proud of the body by about 1/4in (6mm). It will be necessary to repeat this a few times in order to get down to the required depth. Slope the wings back from the tip, contouring them smoothly into the body at about shoulder height with the 3/8in (9mm) No.6 (Fig 29).

Bosting In

This is the stage at which the shaping takes place. The bulk of the wood is removed with the 5/8in (5mm) No.7, although the beak, because of its vulnerability, is best rounded with a medium-cut round rat tail file, while the feet can be left until later. Undercut the edge of the wings with a 1/8in (3mm) No.10 making a shallow cut sufficient to make it appear that the wing is detached from the body at the tip, but not enough to make the wing edges vulnerable to damage. Clean up the whole carving with a scraper paying particular attention to the head which should now be symmetrical when viewed from all angles and which will be dealt with next.

The Head

The eyes lie in a shallow depression which is formed with a 1/4in (6mm) No.9. The depression runs from the centre of the head to the top of the bill

Fig 29

and when cut in also forms the eyebrow and the step at the back of the bill. It can clearly be seen in Fig 31.

The Eyes

The eyes are spheres with small triangles cut in at the corners. The spheres are formed by rotating a suitably-sized gouge, say a 3/16in (4.5mm) No.9 vertically above the eye position. This will cut an accurate circle into the wood which can then be rounded over with a 1/8in (3mm) No.3. The triangles at each corner of the eye can be cut in either with a craft knife or a small firmer chisel. Finish the eye with a small hole made in the centre of the eyeball with the point of a large needle. You will be surprised how this will bring the eye to life. The gape is simply cut in with a 1/16in (1.5mm) No.11. As few carvers are likely to possess this tool when starting off an alternative would be to cut it in by making two angled cuts with a craft knife (Fig 30).

The Feet and the Egg

The feet are webbed with three forward-facing toes. Remove the wood between the feet with a 1/4in (6mm) No.9 and form the two depressions between the toes with a 3/8in (9mm) No.6. The egg is first defined by stabbing in vertically with a 3/8in (9mm) No.6. The waste wood round the edges of the cut is removed with a 3/8in (9mm) No.3, the same gouge being used to round over the egg (Fig 30).

The Base

Sand the base with reducing grades of sandpaper, folding each piece over a square block of wood to keep it flat. The top can be finished by making a series of small cuts across its surface with a flattish gouge, say a 3/16in (4.5mm) No 3. The textured surface so formed will provide a contrast between the polished base sides and the carving. Mark two lines round the base, one round the top about 3/16in (4.5mm) in from the sides and the other on the sides 3/16in (4.5mm) down from the top. Cut in a cove between the two lines with a 1/4in (6mm) No.9 – the irregular hardness of the grain will tend to prevent the gouge running smoothly from one

Fig 30 A view of the carved object; remember the importance of working out your ideas before starting on the carving.

end of the base to the other. This can easily be smoothed out with a round medium-cut rat tail file or a sheet of sandpaper wrapped round a short length of dowel of suitable size.

The Finishing

Clean up the whole work with a scraper and reducing grades of sandpaper. Any rough patches discovered during the sanding can be scraped out and resanded. Lightly dab the whole carving with a damp rag to lift the grain, and

73

Fig 31 The penguin. A side view of the carving of this most endearing of animals.

when thoroughly dry lightly sand with flour-grade sandpaper. Make your mark somewhere on the base and, for added interest, the date.

Rub the whole carving down very vigorously indeed with a soft cloth – this will not only remove the dust but will also burnish the surface wood and improve the final appearance. Seal the wood with varnish or sanding sealer, including the bottom of the base. The varnish will reduce the ingress and regress of water vapour which is a possible cause of future checks. When thoroughly dry again rub down very vigorously indeed with 0 grade steel wool until all the surface varnish has been removed leaving only the grain sealed with varnish. Apply a good quality wax polish and buff lightly with a soft cloth. Repeated applications of the wax polish and the buffing will continue to add to the appearance of the carving.

THE SAILING BOAT PLAQUE (SCALE 1)

This plaque is more straightforward to carve than it might at first sight appear as, unlike most reliefs, practically all the carving is on one level and little account has to be taken of perspective. The circular shape fits in well with the shape of the hull and the sails and the beading moulding done round the edge with a router gives a standard of finish that would be difficult and laborious to achieve by hand. For those carvers who do not possess an electric router, however, a plain edge or one with a simple cove carved round it similar to the one carved round the edge of the penguin base would look fine.

The wood used was a nice clean piece of chestnut (Castanea sativa) but any hardwood would be suitable, although a strongly-figured wood would look better on the curving sails and hull.

As with all carved work consideration must always first be given to holding the wood securely, and above all safely, in the vice. The plaque illustrated was held using the peg board described earlier in the book which leaves the top surface completely clean. G cramps could be used but they are always in the way. An alternative is to glue a softwood block to the back of the plaque which

Fig 32 How the plaque is visualised at an early stage.

will enable it to be held in the vice and, when necessary, turned round in ninety degree steps. Using a softwood block enables it to be split away easily when the carving is finished.

Produce a drawing from the design using the grid to scale up or down to the required size. Mark out the round wood blank with carbon paper fixed underneath the drawing, securing the paper to the wood with Blu-Tack as drawing pins leave unsightly holes.

Lowering the Background

For those who possess an electric router the background can now be routed out and the beading moulding formed round the edge using a beading cutter that has an integral guide.

To lower the background by hand, a channel is first cut round the design about 1/4in (6mm) away from its edge with a 3/8in (9mm) No.10. This channel achieves two objects. Firstly, it provides a relieving cut so that when the edge of the design is cleaned up wood will crumble on the side of the relieving cut giving a crisp clean edge to the design. Secondly, it provides a stop cut for the large bosting in gouge, say a 5/8in (15mm) No.7, which is now used to remove the background wood so preventing the gouge from over-running and cutting into the edge of the design. It will be necessary to repeat this several times in order to reach the required depth. The depth is marked round the side of the wood by holding the pencil normally between the thumb and forefinger. The other fingers are used as guides on the top edge of the wood. This is a quick and accurate method of drawing lines on an irregular or curved surface (Fig 33).

The background can now be levelled with a flatter gouge, say a 5/8in (15mm) No.3, although a small hand router (Fig 3) could be used as an alternative (Fig 34). In this case it would be necessary to leave ridges across the face of the wood the width of the router base apart for the router to rest on. The ridges are cut away when the routing is complete with a 3/8in (9mm) No.6.

The 1/8in (3mm) of wood that has been left round the edge of the design can now be cut away by stabbing down vertically with suitably shaped gouges. The design should then be left standing proud above the cleaned-up background with vertical clean-cut edges.

Fig 33 The finger edge method of drawing an accurate line, using the fingers as a guide.

The Foresail

The three points of the foresail where it connects to the mast and bow are lowered almost to the background with a 3/8in (9mm) No.3, and the three sides of the sail are rounded off, again, almost to the background, with the same tool (Fig 35).

The Mast

Lower the wood of the mast where it contacts the hull very slightly, about 1/16in (1.5mm), and slope the mast back from there until the tip is only just above the background. Define the back of the mast where it contacts the mainsail

Fig 34

and the flag by stabbing down vertically with a firmer chisel, then round both the flag and the sail into this cut with a 3/8in (9mm) No.3. Lower the boom and the spar at the top of the mainsail almost to the background and define them in the same way as the mast, also rounding off the sail into them (Fig 35).

The Flag

The flag should now have been rounded into the mast, so lower the centre with a 1/4in (6mm) No.9 and the tip almost to the background with a 3/8in (9mm) No.3 (Fig 35).

The Hull

Define the top of the waves with a 1/4in (6mm) No.9 and round off the hull into the cut with a 3/8in (9mm) No.3. This will have to be repeated several times in order to reach the required depth, which is almost as deep as the background. The starboard, or right-hand edge of the bow, should also be rounded nearly to the background.

Define each side of the stempost with a small quick gouge, with say, a 3/16in (4.5mm) No.11 and remove the waste wood each side with a 3/8in (9mm) No.3 leaving the stempost standing slightly proud. Round off the bottom of the

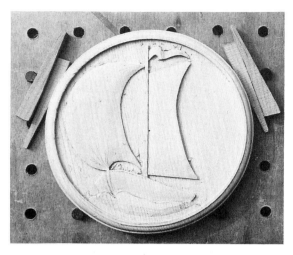

Fig 35

water where it meets the router cut with a 3/8in (9mm) No.3. Define the foam at the stem with the 3/16in (4.5mm) No.11 and remove the waste with a 3/8in (9mm) No.3 leaving the foam proud. Round off the edges of the foam and use a 3/8in (9mm) No.6 to simulate waves with a series of shallow gouge cuts across the water (Fig 36).

Use the 3/16in (4.5mm) No.11 to gouge a small line about 1/8in (3mm) down from the top edge of the hull to define the hull edge clearly and to indicate planking. Round off the mast and spars with the 3/8in (9mm) No.3 and form the gaps between the mast and the mainsail by stabbing down vertically with a suitably shaped gouge, say a 5/8in (15mm) No.7 and then removing the waste with a 3/16in (4.5mm) No.3. Mark in the creases in the sails where they are stretched at the contact points and carve them in with a 1/4in (6mm) No.9 smoothing them over with the 3/8in (9mm) No.3.

Clean up the whole relief with a

scraper, also using it to smoothly round off edges which still have gouge marks left in them. Small scrapers are useful to finish the creases in the sail. Sand with reducing grades of sandpaper, finishing with flour. Now that the background is smooth the seagulls can be carved in by simply making two cuts with a V tool – if one is not available; two inclined cuts with a craft knife will produce the same result.

The beading moulding round the edge looks well without additional decoration but I have carved on to this a simple rope pattern which is appropriate for the subject of the plaque. It may well also be of value for other mouldings that you are considering for the future, for example, round the edge of a crest. It is carved in with a 1/8in (3mm) No.11, the marking out being self-explanatory (Fig 36).

Fig 36 The finished decorative sailing boat plaque.

Finishing

Lightly damp only the readily available flat areas, being careful to avoid areas that cannot be effectively sanded. When dry, rub down with flour paper and, after very vigorously removing all dust, seal with varnish or a sanding sealer (not forgetting the back). Rub down again with well-worn flour paper and then wax polish, using a white wax for a light-coloured wood such as the chestnut that was used for the plaque illustrated (Fig 36).

THE DOLPHIN (SCALE 1)

The dolphin is of the family *Cetacea* which also includes whales and porpoises, all warm-blooded mammals. The superb shape of this beautiful creature lends itself ideally to being depicted in wood, and time taken carefully to select a piece with a suitable grain would be amply repaid. The carving illustrated in Fig 41 was carved in Cornish Elm *(Ulmus stricta)* which is a great favourite of mine. It is not the easiest wood to carve but the rather wild grain, its rich brown colour, and its tough sinewy strength make it a good and attractive general-purpose carving wood which is more forgiving to work with than the more brittle and splintery woods like mahogany. This is a straightforward carving suitable for the inexperienced carver – it will help to build up expertise in the use of tools and the way in which work in the round is approached.

As with the carving of all natural forms, whether animals, birds, plants, or fish, photographs and drawings of the subject should be carefully studied before the carving and at frequent intervals throughout, and where possible notes and sketches should be made of the actual plant or creature. It will be helpful for you to build up a scrapbook of pictures that may be of future use which would include such details as hands or feet, suitable plant forms and so on. Experience quickly teaches you what is likely to be useful, for example, nearly all photographs and drawings of animals illustrate the side view. They rarely show the inelegant but just as useful rear view and yet to the sculptor in wood this is vitally important. Unless you actually happen to have, say, a rhinoceros to hand you will not know what its rear end looks like. Most libraries can now photocopy pages from their books for a few pence and this is a first-class source of suitable material which will also prompt ideas for future carvings.

Blocking In

Produce a template from the side-view drawing and use it to mark out the wood, taking careful note of the grain, as by moving the template a few inches one way or the other you may avoid an unsightly blemish or improve the grain characteristics. Remove wood from outside the lines by sawing in radially at close intervals and then splitting the wood away with a 5/8in (15mm) No.7 and a carver's mallet. By all means use an electric jigsaw or bandsaw for this job if you possess one as there is no merit in hard work just for the sake of it (Fig 38).

It is just possible to hold this work in the vice by means of its base but this is insecure and, when the base

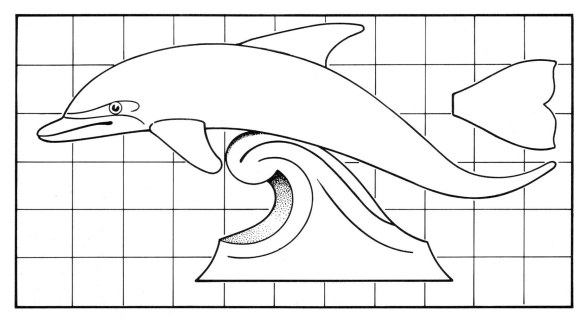

Fig 37 Template for the dolphin carving.

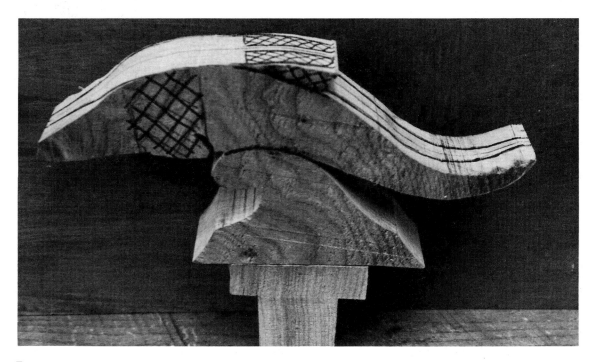

Fig 38

comes to be worked on, inconvenient. A square wood block shaped and screwed to the bottom of the carving, as shown in Fig 38, will be much safer and more convenient. Making the block square will save the time spent opening and closing the vice jaws every time the carving is turned through ninety degrees.

Mark out the area of wood to be temporarily avoided on the side view and also draw in the central fin which is shown by the cross-hatched area in Fig 38. Also mark out the top view as shown in Fig 39. Make a template of the tail and use it to mark out the tail on the top view (Fig 39).

Remove wood from each side of the top fin by first gouging a channel where the fin meets the body with a 3/8in (9mm) No.10, removing the waste wood with a 3/8in (9mm) No.6. It will be necessary to repeat this several times in order to get down to the required depth. The 3/8in (9mm) No.10 will form a radius between the fin and the body which is just about the right shape for this angle.

Remove wood from each side of the body lines with a 5/8in (15mm) No.7. The wood at the rear of the body is more easily removed if a few saw cuts are first made across it, as shown in Fig 39.

Bosting In

The body of the dolphin should now be shaped using the 5/8in (15mm) No.7 avoiding at first the area where the lower side fins will be carved (shown by the cross-hatched area in Fig 38). When the body has been bosted in, the side fins can be carved using the same

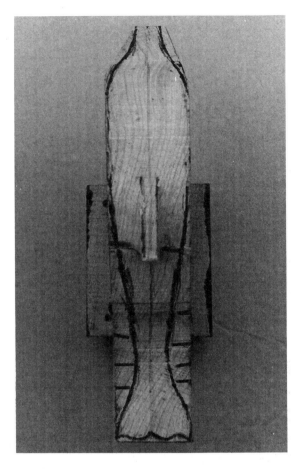

Fig 39 Detail on the dolphin carving; now is the time to decide what effects you are seeking to create.

method as that used to carve the top fin. The wood where the fins meet the body is first lowered with a 3/8in (9mm) No.10, and the waste is removed with a 3/8in (9mm) No.6. The V between the underside of the fins is carved in the same way.

The three fins and the tail should be left approximately 3/16in (4.5mm) thick and a bevel filed on the edges to give the appearance of a thin fin and tail

Fig 40

whilst still retaining plenty of strength. Clean the whole carving up with a round surform; removing the gouge marks with a scraper. This will now enable the surface to be drawn on easily and make you feel better about it all (Fig 40).

The Eye

The eye lies in a depression which is shown in Fig 41. Carve in the depression with a 3/8in (9mm) No.6, rounding the edges off with a medium-cut round rat tail file. The eye can be formed by stabbing down vertically and then rotating a suitably sized and shaped gouge,

say a 3/16in (4.5mm) No.10 in a circle then rounding off the circular cut so formed with a small flat gouge 1/8in (3mm) No.3. An easier way to form a small sphere like this is to drill a shallow hole in the end of a short length of rod of a suitable diameter, about 3/16in (4.5mm). This will form an accurate sphere when pushed firmly into the wood. Finish the eye off by drilling a small hole in the centre of the eyeball with a large needle. A three-sided sailmaker's needle will be ideal for this. It is also a useful tool to keep in the workshop for many other small jobs.

Fig 41 The impression of motion is created in the beautiful carving of the dolphin by placing the subject on the crest of a wave.

The Base

The base takes the form of a stylised wave and looks very effective when finished. It supports the carving securely without any tendency to topple over and it both complements the dolphin and gives an impression of speed. These points are worth noting when designing future carvings. Mark in the cross-hatched area on the wave, shown in Fig 40, and remove the waste wood with a 3/8in (9mm) No.6. Using a medium-cut half round file, file round the back of the wave in the same manner and with the same tools, and mark in the three decorative gouge cuts (Fig 41). Form the three decorative gouge cuts with a 3/8in (9mm) No.10, repeating this a few times in order to reach the required depth and width.

Finishing

Sand the whole carving down with reducing grades of sandpaper, finishing with flour paper, and scrape out any rough areas which have been identified by sanding. Lightly damp the wood to raise the grain and, when thoroughly dry again, rub down with well-worn flour paper. Seal the whole work with varnish or sanding sealer and then rub it down very vigorously with 0 grade steel wool. Finish with repeated applications of a good quality wax polish, lightly buffed with a soft clean duster.

THE HERON (SCALE 1)

Family Ardeidae

This stylised heron carving is based upon the common heron *Arden cinerea cinerea*, which is a particularly elegant and beautiful bird. It is a resident of Britain, being joined in the autumn by large numbers of migrants from the Continent. Its food consists of a large range of small living creatures such as fish, eels, rats, mice, frogs, small birds and so on, which it stabs, sometimes

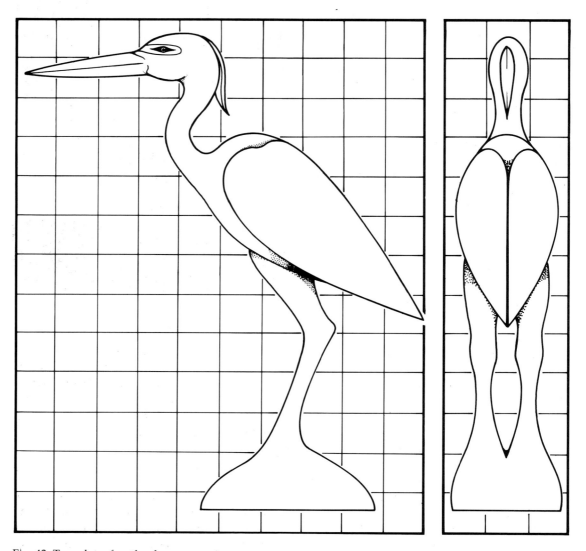

Fig 42 Template for the heron carving.

repeatedly, with its long, pointed, murderous bill. Not all herons are aquatic though. The cattle egret *Bubulcus ibis* spends most of its time on the back of large mammals such as buffaloes and elephants, where it picks off and consumes large numbers of irritating insects, much to the satisfaction of the carrier. It also provides its ride with a warning system, taking flight at the slightest sign of danger.

The heron was once regarded in this country as a suitable target for the peregrine falcon in falconry. Fortunately this danger has largely passed, although, as with so many lovely, living creatures, the heron's habitat is rapidly being destroyed by man, and possibly its harsh cry, or the great boom of the bittern, will no longer be heard in the English countryside.

Blocking In

This carving can quite reasonably be held in the vice by means of its base and was in fact carved in that manner, but a wood block screwed to the bottom would be of assistance, particularly in the later stages when it becomes necessary to work on the base. Produce a template from the side-view drawing and use it to mark out the wood. Remove wood from outside the lines with a 5/8in (15mm) No.7 and carver's mallet, cleaning up the ragged outline with a round surform. Mark on the back and front views after first drawing on a centre line which will help in getting the outline symmetrical.

Remove wood from outside the lines, initially with the 5/8in (15mm) No.7, then remove the bulk of the wood from the beak and the head with a round

Fig 43

surform to avoid damage at this vulnerable point. Note that up to the end of this stage no attempt has been made to shape or round off the carving, the sides having been left flat and the edges at right angles (Fig 43).

Bosting In

This is the point at which the carving is actually shaped so constant references to photographs and drawings of herons will be of great assistance in producing a lively and interesting work. As the shaping takes place the clean-cut outlines

85

disappear and the work tends to become ragged and confused. This is the point in every carving when we all despair, but you will find that once the bulk of the wood has been removed with the 5/8in (15mm) No.7, and the carving has been cleaned up with a round surform, your confidence will be restored. As with the blocking in it is better to shape the head and the beak with the round surform using a medium-cut rat tail file for the final shaping and cleaning up. The wood between the legs should not be removed until the head and wings

Fig 44

are finished in order to retain strength in the legs (Fig 44).

The Wings and Crest

Mark on the wings and crest as shown in Fig 44 and define them with a 1/4in (6mm) No.9. Remove the waste wood from below the wings to make them stand out from the body with a 3/8in (9mm) No.3. The waste wood each side of the crest should also be removed using the same tool, leaving the crest about 3/16in (4.5mm) wide. A shallow depression should also be carved down the centre of the back with a 3/8in (9mm) No.6 to divide the two wings. The edges are rounded over and smoothed off with a file (Fig 45).

The Head

The eyes lie in a depression which runs from the centre of the head to the top of the base of the bill (Fig 46). This depression forms the rather severe-looking eyebrow and the step between the front of the head and the base of the bill. Carve in the depression with a 1/4in (6mm) No.9, gently rounding the edges off with a medium-cut rat tail file. The eyes are formed by stabbing down vertically on the edge of the eyeball with a quick gouge, say a 3/16in (4.5mm) No.10, then cutting in horizontally with the same tool to remove a chip from each side of the eyeball. Drill a small hole in the centre of the eyeball with a large needle for a piercing look.

The Gape

The gape is simply defined with a 1/16in (1.5mm) No.10. If this tool is not available

Fig 45

to find later that more needs to be removed from the external shape – of course it is then too late to do this. Round off the legs with files, using strips of sandpaper pulled back and forth with two hands, for the final small amount of shaping and smoothing. Fix sticky tape or masking tape to the back of the strips of sandpaper to prevent it breaking (Fig 46).

Round over the edges of the crest with a 3/8in (9mm) No.3 and make a few random cuts down it with a 1/16in (1.5mm) No.10 to indicate the long crest feathers (Fig 45). To keep this carving straightforward and therefore suitable for the inexperienced carver it was finished at this point. Much more could

two inclined cuts with a craft knife would also do the job.

The Legs

Shape the exterior of the legs with a round surform ensuring that the shape is correct before attempting to remove wood from between them. This is a good principle to remember for future carvings as so often I have found that my students, in their anxiety to get on and see the final shape appearing, remove wood from between areas only

Fig 46 Side view of the elegant carved heron.

have been done by a more experienced carver to make the bird more realistic. For example, the large webbed feet of the heron could be carved into the base without detracting from the strength of the legs, simple gouge cuts could have been made up the base to indicate reeds, or the wings could have had feathers carved on to them, so with a little thought and extra work you can produce an individual carving instead of a direct copy, which should always be avoided wherever possible. Carve your mark and the date on the base.

Finishing

Unlike most carved wood this carving lends itself well to a highly polished finish and the uncluttered lines make it simple to clean up before the varnish is applied. Scrape out all the remaining gouge marks, rub down with reducing grades of sandpaper and damp before the final sanding as described for previous carvings. The highly polished surface is produced by repeated applications of wax polish (Fig 46).

THE NAMEBOARD (SCALE 2)

The skills and tools required to carve lettering, although similar to those needed for the carving of the previous designs in this book, are, however, different and will provide a valuable extension to the experience and skills already acquired. For those carvers who may wish to profit from their craft there is always a good return for well-designed and well-executed nameboards.

Lettering

The design of nameboards centres on the lettering, so the size and type should be the first thing to be considered. As a very rough rule of thumb lower-case letters between 2–2 1/2in (51–64mm) high, with 3–3 1/2in (77–89mm) capitals, are a good compromise, with the lettering being visible over a reasonable distance but not large enough to make the board bulky and unbalanced. Lettering smaller than 1in (25mm) is very difficult to carve and should not be considered until some experience has been gained.

There is a vast range of alphabets to choose from, although not all of them are suitable for carving. The one most commonly used is Trajan Roman which is taken from an inscription carved on a monument in Rome to the Roman emperor, Trajan. It is generally considered to be the most beautiful and perfectly proportioned lettering that has ever been designed and good examples of it can be seen on public buildings everywhere. For the inexperienced carver, however, Trajan Roman is an unforgiving alphabet, the slightest error showing up badly and affecting the appearance of the whole work. At first, therefore, a less demanding alphabet should be used, the Trajan Roman being left until some experience in letter carving is gained.

Text, or 'Black Letter' as it is also known, pre-dates printing and was the result of the need to compress as much writing on to a sheet of paper as possible, due to the paper's expense and bulk. The black of the writing often overbalanced the white of the paper, hence the name. It looks and harmonises well with old property or church carving

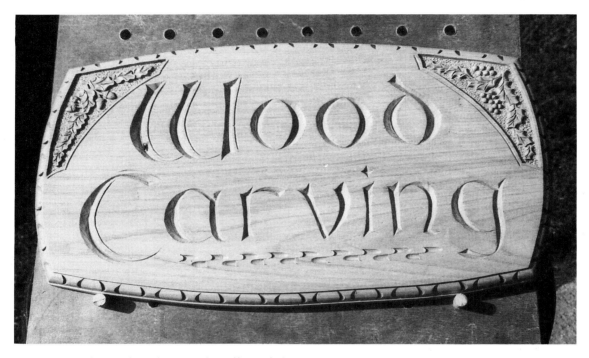

Fig 47 Carved nameboard. Note the effect of the simple chip carved ovolo moulding.

and is usually carved with firmer chisels rather than a V tool or gouges.

The Uncial alphabet is based upon the circle and is attractive and straightforward to carve. It is also suitable for a much wider range of applications than either Trajan Roman or Black Letter and if any slight mistake is made in the carving due to inexperience it can generally be corrected fairly easily.

It is usual for the experienced carver to draw out the lettering straight on to the wood but for the beginner it will be easier to draw the lettering and any decorative carving on to paper first. The size of wood available, particularly the width, often limits the size of the lettering, any decoration and the external shape. Where sufficient wood is available

a sheet of paper which is obviously too large should be folded horizontally and vertically. These two folds are used to assist in centralising the lettering and also, when the lettering has been drawn out, to enable an accurate external shape to be cut out when it is folded in two.

Obtain a copy of the Uncial alphabet, (the local library is a good source) and draw the name out roughly on the paper after first drawing in the guide lines. Start with the centre letter of the name on the vertical centre-fold, followed by the other letters each side of it, working outwards. Remember that if the capital is to be larger than the lower-case letters the centre of the name will be a little to the right to allow for the extra width. The spacing must be judged by eye as there are no rules; this is quite difficult. It is usually necessary to redraw the whole thing out several times before getting it right. Once the spacing and balance are correct the lettering can be drawn in accurately. The external shapes of the circular letters are formed with a compass, and it is then a simple matter to draw in the internal shapes by hand. Not all examples of the Uncial alphabet are suitable for carving and it may be necessary to modify the one that you have obtained to make it suitable or even more attractive. For example the straight verticals which normally have parallel sides could be slightly curved as in the lettering on the nameboards shown in Figs 47, 48(a) and 48(b) or any other modification that may suggest itself to you, provided it does not destroy the legibility of the lettering or become over-fussy.

Once the name has been correctly drawn the external shape of the board should be considered. An oblong or square board can be quite satisfactory and, where the width of the available wood is the limiting factor, these are probably the only shapes possible. However, a curved or shaped board will look much more attractive. The desired shape should be drawn on, allowing sufficient width of wood to rout on the moulding round the edge of the board as well as space to take the two mounting screws at each end. The paper can now be folded on the vertical and horizontal folds and the external outline cut round with scissors on the quarter segment showing. When the paper is opened out the external shape should be accurately centred round the name.

Decoration

Any decorative carving should be designed to ensure that it harmonises with, and does not overwhelm, the lettering and where possible is appropriate. For example, the carved sprigs of holly growing out of the water of the brook have a symbolical significance (if not a strictly accurate botanical one), for the nameboard for Hollybrook House (Fig 48(a)) and similarly for the very stylised thistle carving on the nameboard for Kilmaveonaia (Fig 48(b)). (For those who fail to recognise the word I am assured that it is of Scottish origin.)

The spandrels carved in the two top corners of the other nameboard (Fig 47) are an excellent way of filling the rather large blank spaces which are inevitable when two words of an uneven length form the name. In this case the relief carvings of stylised oak and holly have no direct connection with the wording, although I feel that they fit the subject very well. The spandrels on a board intended for a mariner could have a mermaid carved in one and perhaps a seahorse in the other, or animals' heads for a farmer or pet lover. Incidentally, shallow relief spandrels like this look extremely good carved on the four corners of a coffee table, and they will not affect the stability of the crockery if the elements of the design are sufficiently close together and the relief carving is very shallow.

Chip carving can also be used to good effect for the decoration of nameboards, either to underline a name or to decorate a moulding as in the case of the 'Wood Carving' board (Fig 47). It may be felt that the decorative chip carving on this board was overdone and unnecessary

(a)

(b)

Fig 48(a) and (b) An additional interest is given to any decorative carving on a nameboard if it is associated with the name. For example, the Scotch thistle motif adds to the effect of the Kilmaveonia board, and the holly growing from the brook similarly enhances the Hollybrook board.

but it was only carved to illustrate a point and to indicate a decorative method that may be of use for future carvings. It is worth noting that the inner edges of the spandrels and the capital letters have a narrow line gouged round them, as has the edge of the cove routed round the Kilmaveonaia board (Figs 47, 48(b) and 50). This is a quick, simple and effective way of emphasising an edge which would not otherwise stand out clearly on its own.

Woods

With the design completed the wood should be planed and sanded to a good standard of finish. This will reveal any faults that may exist which can then be avoided and also allow the design to stand out clearly when it is drawn on the board. This is essential for accurate working.

The wood used for each of the boards illustrated was chestnut, *Castanea sativa,* its light yellow colour contrasting sharply with the dark shadows cast by the lettering. It carves crisply and stands well outside. Any wood could be used but for outside use care should be taken to select a wood that will weather attractively and resist rot. Oak, chestnut, elm, iroko and teak are good examples. Parana pine, although perhaps not quite as attractive as these woods, has the advantage that it can be bought in standard 10in (25cm) widths as it is normally used for staircase treads.

When wood is carved on one surface only, as in the case of a relief, it tends to curl towards the carved side. This effect can be resisted by using a suitable thickness of wood, 1 1/4in (31mm) is about ideal, and by arranging the carving to be on the opposite side to the natural curl of the wood. This can be determined by viewing the end of the plank, which may already have a slight curl; if it doesn't, the natural curl will be opposite to the curve of the annual rings.

Use the design to mark out the external shape of the board, saw it out and clean up and sand the edges before any moulding is routed round the edge. Ensure that the ends of the design centre lines are marked on the ends of the board so that when necessary the design can be accurately relocated.

Screw or glue a square, softwood block on to the bottom of the board to enable it to be held securely in the vice; alternatively the peg board illustrated in Fig 10 could be used.

Moulding

An edge moulding is not essential but it does give an attractive, professional finish to the work and is well worth considering. Mouldings can be worked by hand but compared with the speed and accuracy of the electric router this is too time-consuming (although a simple cove can be quickly carved and look quite well). In addition, mouldings can themselves be carved as in the simple chip-carved beading moulding surrounding the 'Wood Carving' board (Fig 47). If a moulding has been decided upon it should now be routed round the edge of the board using a cutter with an integral guide pin, or alternatively carved by hand.

Secure the four corners of the design paper to the board using Blu-Tack rather than drawing pins which leave unsightly holes. Mark out the design on the wood using carbon paper; a ballpoint pen will leave a more positive mark than a pencil and enable you to see which parts of the design have already been traced. Once the design is marked out on the wood it should be examined for balance and spacing before the carving is started as at this stage it can easily be altered. It may also be possible to make use of some attractive feature of the grain which up to now has been overlooked. Many years ago I made a name for myself as a wood carver when I carved a relief of a local church to be presented to a lady. At the presentation several people said to me how clever I had been to use the grain radiating from a knot in the wood to appear to light up the church. With all due humility I readily agreed, although it wasn't until I had had a second look that I realised what they meant!

Carving

The Uncial alphabet can be carved using

the same method as that used to carve Trajan Roman. In this method a centre line is first stabbed vertically down to a depth of approximately 1/8in (3mm), using a firmer chisel for the straight sections of the letter and gouges with a suitable sweep for the curved sections. Two inclined cuts are then made into the central cut thus removing a V-shaped chip. The serifs, if any, are cut in with an almost flat fishtail gouge, say a 3/8in (9mm) No.3. I have, however, found that it is quicker and easier to carve the Uncial alphabet, which is mainly rounded forms, with a 3/8in (9mm) 60° V tool using either a 1/4in (6mm) firmer chisel or a craft knife for the serifs. Whichever method is used it is important to understand that when a gouge or V tool enters the wood the fibres are forced apart and this tends to leave a ragged surface. This effect can be overcome by making a relieving cut along the centre line of the letter with the V tool as shown in Fig 49, then on the next cut the wood will crumble on the side of the relieving cut, leaving a cleaner and crisper surface to the sides of the letters. This relieving cut also enables the carver to determine which side of the V tool is cutting smoothly and which side is tearing the grain. On the next cut, which will be out to the edges of the letter, the V tool can be biased to cut on the smooth side only, and then reversed to cut smoothly down the other side. The

Fig 49 The relieving cut, made with a 3/8in (9mm) No. 10 V tool. This prevents the edges of the letters crumbling and indicates in which direction the final cuts should be made in order to produce a clean crisp edge.

depth of the cut varies with the width of the letter, the deepest part being at the widest part of the letter progressively reducing out to the serifs. The serifs can be cut in with a 1/4in (6mm) firmer chisel or a craft knife.

The thin, gouged line made round the inside edges of the capitals for emphasis is cut in with a 1/8in (3mm) No.10.

Chip Carving

The chip carving that is used to underline the word 'Carving' (Fig 47) is simply and quickly carved, first by stabbing down vertically with a 1/4in (6mm) No.9 and then cutting in horizontally with the same gouge until the chip comes cleanly away. All the chips in this particular pattern are of equal length. This simple basic method can be used to form geometric patterns or decorative stylised flowers which are a very effective form of decoration, particularly in a good side light. The chip carving used to decorate the beading moulding is carved in exactly the same way but this time using a much larger gouge, say a 5/8in (15mm) No.7, and with the horizontal cuts only being inclined instead of horizontal. When marking out this pattern on to the moulding it will be easier to mark in the four corners first, spacing the rest of the cuts evenly between them.

Oak-Leaved Spandrels

The method used to carve the spandrels is the same as for any other relief carving. The design and the edges of the spandrels are first outlined with a small quick gouge, say a 3/16in (4.5mm) No.10 about 1/8in (3mm) away from the edge of the relief and the edge of the spandrel. The waste wood between the cuts is removed with a 3/16in (4.5mm) No.3. The depth of the background need only be very shallow for this relief, about 3/16in (4.5mm). The 3/16in (4.5mm) No.10 can now be used to remove the last 1/8in (3mm) of wood right up to the edges of the spandrels. The edges of the design can be shaped by stabbing down vertically with suitably shaped gouges. Incidentally, it is good practice when designing a relief to ensure as far as possible that its shape fits the sweeps of the available gouges. This makes the stabbing down much quicker and easier and saves the difficulty of trying to nibble away at an outline with gouges whose sweeps do not quite fit the design.

The design should now be standing about 3/16in (4.5mm) above the background with its external shape accurately defined and with vertical sides. The second stage of any relief carving is to determine the level of each element of the design and reduce them accordingly. This does not apply in this case, however, in which it is only necessary to indicate where one leaf covers another by cutting round the tip of the higher leaf where it joins the lower with a quick gouge and then reducing the tip of the lower leaf with a 1/4in (6mm) No.3 (Fig 50).

Modelling

This is where the top surfaces of the leaves are shaped and the acorns rounded over. This stage is equivalent to the bosting in of a work in the round. Carve the top surfaces of the leaves with a 3/8in (9mm) No.6 to make them irregular, reducing the lower parts of

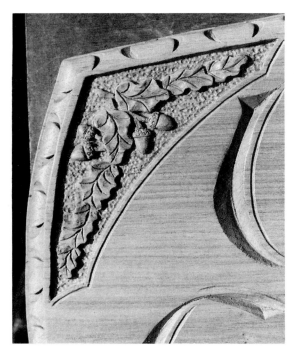

Fig 50 The oak spandrel attractively fills a gap left by the uneven wording and could also be used to decorate the edges of a coffee table.

the irregularities almost down to the background to get as much movement into the carving as possible. Round over some of the leaf tips almost to the background with a 1/4in (6mm) No.3 in ways that naturally suggest themselves to you, then draw in the veining and define with a V tool. If a V tool is not available the veins can be cut in with two inclined cuts with a craft knife (Fig 50). The cups of the acorns are covered with small dimples which can be formed by drilling a shallow spherical hole in the end of a length of 1/8in (3mm) rod, a nail with the end ground flat will do. This will produce the dimples when pushed with some force at close intervals into the acorn cup.

The background was textured by tapping a nail with a rounded end at close intervals into the surface. The texturing provides a sharp contrast between the elements of the design and the background, making it stand out more sharply. You may think it necessary to carve the background down to an exact depth all over, this being one of the advantages of the router, but in fact a completely flat machine-like level surface is not always desirable. It is often an advantage to deepen some elements of the design more than others.

Holly Spandrels

The holly spandrel is carved in exactly the same way as the oak spandrel with the exception of the holly berries. These are carved by first stabbing down vertically with a suitably sized and shaped gouge, say a 1/4in (6mm) No.9, and then sliding the gouge round until the circle is complete. The sweep of the gouge must be part of the circumference of a circle, as opposed to a No.10 or 11 which are U—shaped and so would not form a circle. The berries can be rounded off with a 1/8in (3mm) No.3.

Emphasise the inner edges of the spandrels with a thin gouged line carved with a 1/8in (3mm) No.10 (Fig 50).

Finishing

Sand down with reducing grades of sandpaper, being careful to avoid the crisply carved edges of any decorative carving. The board can either be oiled, which will give it some measure of protection, or varnished. In the case of varnish it is important to use one formulated for use outside, containing an ultra-violet barrier. The back of the board must also be varnished. If the board is to be positioned where the light is defused with little or no side light to form shadows it may be necessary to paint the lettering to make it stand out, although this should be avoided if at all possible. I have found that car touch-up paint retains its colour well – particularly white, which is the colour most often used – and also dries rapidly. The paint should be applied after the board has been varnished as it is then possible to remove any paint that almost inevitably strays over the edge of the lettering on to the top surface of the board cleanly.

Nameboards are normally supported with a countersunk screw situated at each end of the board. The resulting screw holes are unsightly, particularly if the screws rust, causing a black stain. One solution is to countersink the screw heads well down into the board and fit in a rosette to conceal the screw.

The rosette can easily be fashioned from a piece of dowel made from the same wood as the board. Its diameter should be about 1/4in (6mm) larger than the screw hole. The section of dowel that fits in the screw holes can be wasted with a file or turned in an electric drill, the remaining wood rounded over and then crossed with two V cuts made with a triangular file to form the head of the rosette.

THE OTTER (SCALE 2)

Lutra (lutra)

Unremitting and relentless persecution by man, despite protection in law, has reduced the numbers of these enchanting creatures to the stage where the banks of nearly all the rivers and streams in this country are deserted. Largely nocturnal, the otter is also mainly aquatic, living on frogs, eels, waterfowl, fish and many other fresh and salt water creatures. It does, without doubt, take some trout and salmon, which is the cause of much of its persecution but some would feel that this is a very small price to pay for the pleasure and excitement that this beautiful wild creature can give to the very fortunate observer.

The otter's coat is chocolate brown in colour, very dense and waterproof, with a smooth appearance when the animal is dry. It is sufficient, therefore, when finishing the carving, to allow the grain of the wood to indicate the texturing of the hair and if a chocolate brown wood is chosen for the work, such as Brazilian mahogany, iroko, teak, or the heartwood of elm, it will add to the realism of the work.

This pose was chosen for a number of reasons. In the first place it is very characteristic of all members of the weasel family, of which the otter is one of the largest members – the vertical stance supported by the thick strong tail enables the animal to peer over the top of large clumps of vegetation. The pose is also right for wood in that there are no thin vulnerable sections to be broken, with even the tail and the front feet forming part of the solid block. For those carvers who want to do other otter carvings after this one, there are many poses which would be just as suitable and characteristic of the animal. For example, the playful habit the otter has of making itself a slide in either mud or snow, would provide some very

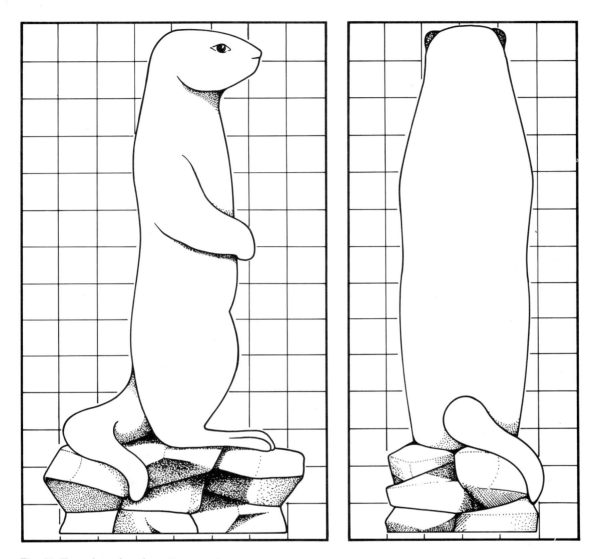

Fig 51 Template for the otter carving.

fine studies, or the sea otter, lying on its back, cracking open a sea shell with a stone, would be another possibility. For the more experienced carver, this basic, straighforward carving could easily be refined by the addition of a fine plump fish lying across the rocks or in the otter's hands. Remember, though, that the otter, unlike other fish-eating animals, eats its fish from the tail first — a fact that led to my downfall in the early days of my carving when the work was examined by a very knowing countryman. A little thought before the work commences will produce a more exciting, individual, and rewarding carving.

Blocking In

Produce a template from the side-view drawing using the grid to scale up or down to fit the available wood. Thoroughly clean up the wood by either planing or sanding. This will enable any small faults such as cracks to be noted that would otherwise go undetected until the carving had been started. Screw a wood block to the bottom of the base to enable the work to be held securely in the vice. Use the template to mark out the cleaned-up block of wood. Remove wood from outside the lines by sawing in radially at close intervals

and then splitting the waste wood away with a 5/8in (15mm) No.7 and a wood carver's mallet. Clean up the ragged outlines which are left with a round surform; a bandsaw or electric jigsaw would, of course, be much quicker and cleaner. Carve the tail, where it curves over the rocks, very deeply indeed with a 3/8in (9mm) No.10. This will ensure that it is not forgotten later when the rocks come to be carved (Fig 52). Draw on the external views of the front and back, which incidentally are the same, and remove the wood from outside the lines with the 5/8in (15mm) No.7 (Fig 53).

Fig 52

Fig 53

Fig 54

Bosting In

Shape the carving, removing the bulk of waste with a 5/8in (15mm) No.7 and then using a 3/8in (9mm) No.6 for the final shaping. Obtain and carefully study photographs of otters throughout this stage of the carving to give added life and realism. Note that the ears, which are very small and almost concealed by fur, are easily overlooked during the shaping of the head and that the tail curves smoothly over the rocks. Another point to watch is to ensure that the body and tail are very round indeed.

The tendency is just to round over the square corners, leaving the body too square (Fig 52).

The Rocks

To enable the area round the bottom of the tail and feet to be accurately defined the rocks should now be drawn in and carved in ways that naturally suggest themselves to you. Use the drawings and Fig 55 as a guide. Any modification to the design that you may have decided upon, such as a fish lying across the rocks, should also be drawn in and defined.

The cracks separating the rocks are defined very deeply with a 3/8in (9mm) No.10, repeating the cut several times in order to achieve a good depth. Make the rocks as irregular as possible by sloping some down into others with a 3/8in (9mm) No.6. Fig 55 will make this clear.

The Head

Although the head looks simple to carve compared with a horse's head for example, its shape is in fact very subtle, and a careful study of photographs is necessary to achieve the sharp, intelligent, cheeky look that is so characteristic of the otter. Note that the head is very broad, being about as wide as the body.

The Ears

The ears are almost concealed by the deep fur but are more evident in the rear and front views than the side view. Carve in the ears with a 1/4in (6mm) No.9, rounding them over and finally shaping them with a medium-cut rat tail file. The depression in the centre of the ears is very shallow and is best carved in with a 1/8in (3mm) No.3.

The Eyes

The eyes are small but well defined and lie in a shallow depression that also forms the lower line of the eyebrow. Carve in the depression with a 1/4in (6mm) No.9 and round over the lower line of the eyebrow with a medium-cut rat tail file (Fig 55).

Form the eye either by stabbing vertically down with a suitably shaped gouge or a length of rod which has had a shallow depression drilled in the end as has been described for previous carvings. Give it its sharp, piercing look by drilling a small hole in the centre of the eyeball with the point of a large needle. This hole gives the same effect as the dab of light-coloured paint used by the artist to highlight an eye.

The Nose

The nostrils could be carved in with a small quick gouge, say a 1/16in (1.5mm) No.10 but this tool is rarely available in the beginner's tool kit and the wood on each side of the cut can easily crumble unless great care is taken. On balance it would be easier to cut in the nostrils with two inclined cuts with a craft knife (Fig 55).

The Mouth

The mouth in most views is barely perceptible. Any attempt to carve it in can result in a rather unpleasant rodent-like look quite foreign to the otter. It can be ignored altogether without detracting from the appearance or the realism of the head.

The Front Feet

The shoulders and arms are covered with thick waterproof fur and are very wide indeed, narrowing down rapidly to the thin wrist and webbed front feet. It is again very characteristic of the otter that in this pose the front feet are held in the position shown in Fig 55. The five claws and the depressions between the toes are barely visible due to the dense fur.

The Rear Feet

The rear feet are webbed with five toes. Carve in the depression between the toes using a 3/16in (4.5mm) No.6 and round off the very short length of leg that is visible outside the fur.

The Base

The base, which should already have been roughly carved to allow the bottom of the tail and the rear feet where they meet the base to be defined, should now be finished and cleaned up. Leave a smooth, clear space on one of the rocks for the carver's mark and the date which should now be carved in.

Finishing

Scrape out all the remaining gouge marks and rough areas and then sand down with reducing grades of sandpaper, finishing with flour. The sanding will identify rough areas which had not been obvious before. These should be scraped out or, in severe cases, recut with gouges

Fig 55 This attractively carved otter captures the sharp and alert look of the creature effectively.

surface with varnish or sanding sealer, including the bottom of the base. When thoroughly dry rub down again very vigorously with 0 grade steel wool until all the obvious traces of varnish have been removed.

Apply a good quality wax polish and buff up with a soft clean duster, repeating until a lovely soft, lustrous polish has been worked up.

THE GRAPE PLAQUE (SCALE 2)

Acanthus foliage and the vine are the two plant forms that have influenced European carvers more than any other. The large, strongly outlined leaf of the acanthus which would have been readily available to the medieval carvers is an obvious choice for the wood carver. The vine also has a strongly-outlined, handsome leaf with the bunches of grapes and twisted stems providing an added interest. The choice of the vine, particularly for church carving, follows from a quotation of the words of Jesus 'I am the vine and ye are the branches'. These words have led to a wealth of carving in which the vine has been depicted in every conceivable form. Most churches possess finely-carved examples done many centuries ago with only a few crude simple tools.

The study of these carvings and the fascinating stories behind them will suggest subjects to carve and ways in which to carve them that could not otherwise be imagined. Some years ago I was commissioned to carve a figure for the church of St Newlina at Newlyn East, Cornwall. Legend has it that St Newlina was a young and beautiful

as it is seldom possible to clean them up with sandpaper alone. A quicker alternative that might be considered is to use a flap-wheel fitted in an electric drill. This will sand the carving, particularly the base which is difficult to sand, much more quickly and if care is taken will not sand over crisply-carved edges.

When the sanding is complete, rub down the carving very vigorously with a clean cloth to remove the sawdust and to impart a burnished glow to the surface of the wood, thus providing a good surface for the varnish. Seal the

Fig 56 Template for the bunch of grapes plaque.

Celtic princess who, during her journeying through Cornwall spreading the word of the Gospel, decided to rest awhile at St Newlyn East. As she plunged her staff into the ground it sprang to life and sprouted into a fig tree. It was on this spot many centuries ago that she built her church and, quite extraordinarily, the fig tree still survives to this day, growing out of the solid stonework of the church with no obvious root system to support it. Legends surrounding the old tree say that anybody who trims or attempts to destroy it will be struck dead and there is some evidence to suggest that in the past this has been the case. Few people today believe these old legends, of course, and many would undertake the task of trimming it, as I would myself, but unfortunately we never seem to quite have the time!

To illustrate a point the outside edge of the plaque was left plain, with the exception of a 3/8in (9mm) wide smooth border, and not routed with moulding cutters. The border was lowered about 1/8in (3mm) below the background of the plaque with a 1/2in (12mm) firmer chisel. The smooth polished finish contrasts sharply with the textured background. For those carvers without a router this is a simple and effective way to finish the edges of plaques and nameboards. It was common practice in the past to allow some elements of the design, such as the tip of a leaf or a stem, to stray naturally over the edge of the border. Those carvers who wish to make their carvings individual may like to do this or add the curly tendrils that support the vine which could be easily incised into the background with a very small quick gouge.

The wood used for carving this relief was chestnut *Castanea sativa*, which carves crisply and although nicely figured does not dominate the detail. Any hardwood could be successfully used however.

Produce a drawing, scaled up or down to fit the available stock, and transfer it to the carefully cleaned-up surface of the wood with carbon paper. Emphasise any weak outlines that may be left when the carbon paper is removed with a soft 2B pencil – it is important for accurate working that all outlines should be clear and sharp. Incidentally, pencil marks on wood can easily be removed with a pencil eraser. It seems an obvious point to make but it is surprising how many students I see trying to remove them with files or sandpaper only to succeed in rubbing the graphite into the surrounding wood and leaving a grubby mark. It will be found necessary only to draw in the external outline of the bunch of grapes at this stage, instead of each individual grape.

Blocking In

Screw or glue a square block of softwood approximately 3×3×1in (77×77×25mm) thick securely to the centre of the bottom of the plaque to enable it to be held firmly in the vice, or use the peg board previously described. Gouge in a stop cut with a 3/8in (9mm) No.10 round the edge of the design approximately 1/8in (3mm) away from its edge (Fig 57). Mark in the depth of the background round the edge of the plaque and lower the background by gouging in from the edge to the stop cut with a 5/8in (15mm) No.7 (Fig 57). Repeat this several times in order to achieve the required depth,

 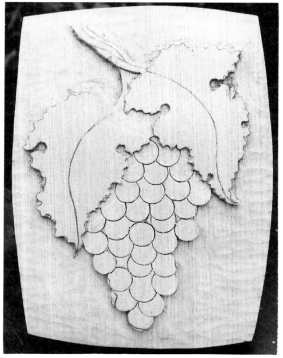

Fig 57 Note the relieving cut made round the design. This reduces the risk of the design crumbling and provides a stop cut to prevent the grounding tool over running into the design.

Fig 58 Use a suitably shaped gouge to stab down vertically when defining the grapes. It is unnecessary to follow the drawing exactly.

keeping all the cuts as even as possible. Stab vertically down round the edges of the design with suitably shaped gouges to remove the last 1/8in (3mm) of wood and to give a crisp vertical edge to it (Fig 58).

Bosting In

The Leaves

Shape the leaves with a 3/8in (9mm) No.6 in ways that naturally suggest themselves to you. For example, round the tip of one leaf over nearly to the background whilst leaving the tip of the other leaf raised, then lower the area of wood immediately in from the tip

almost to the background to give the appearance of a turned-up tip. See the right-hand leaf in Figs 59 and 60. Deeply cut in the central vein of each leaf with a 3/8in (9mm) 60° V tool, repeating several times in order to reach the required depth which is about the same depth as the background. Smoothly round over the edges of the V tool cut with a 3/8in (9mm) No.3 and scrape out all gouge marks leaving a smooth round surface to each leaf (Fig 59). Mark in all the veins, curving them smoothly from the edge of the leaf into the central vein. This will serve to emphasise the shape of the leaf and give a deceptive appearance of depth. Cut in the veins with a 3/8in (9mm) 60° V tool (Fig 60). A smaller tool would be desirable but

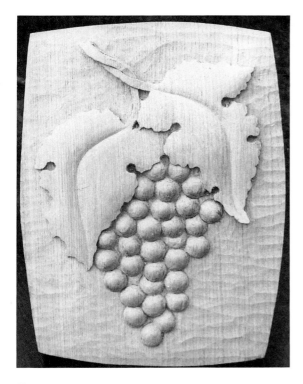

Fig 59

gouge, say a 3/8in (9mm) No.3 repeating several times in order to get down to the required depth (Fig 59).

The Stems

Carving the twist in the stems looks tricky but is really quite simple. Pencil in the twist in the stems (Fig 58) and stab down vertically at the point where one stem crosses over another with a suitably shaped gouge – a 3/8in (9mm) No.3 should fit nicely. Use the same gouge to remove the wasted wood from each side of the higher stem, cutting into the vertical cut already made and ensuring that one stem flows smoothly over and under the other (Fig 59). Lastly round over the stems with the 3/8in (9mm) No.3 (Fig 60).

The Base

Clean up and level the background with a 3/8in (9mm) No.6 by making a series of small regular cuts across its surface. At the same time these cuts can be used to texture the surface attractively and will provide a sharp contrast between the design and the background so making the design stand out clearly. The background should be as flat and level as possible although at certain points, for example below the raised leaf tip, it could be lowered slightly in order to emphasise the turned-up tip effectively.

Pencil a line approximately 3/8in (9mm) from the edge of the base and remove wood down to a depth of about 1/8in (3mm) with a 1/2in (12mm) firmer chisel, smoothing the chiselled surface off afterwards with a medium-cut flat file and sandpaper. This simply formed edge could have been routed with an

when only one is available, which is usually the case in the beginner's kit, the 3/8in (9mm) V will cope with a much larger range of work than the smaller tool.

The Grapes

Use a suitably shaped gouge whose sweep forms part of the circumference of a circle, say a 5/8in (15mm) No.7, to stab down vertically round the edge of each grape, and move the gouge round after each cut until the circle is complete (Fig 58). It is advisable not to pencil in the shape of each individual grape as the pencilled outline rarely accurately fits the sweep of the gouge. It is better to stab down on the unmarked surface, each grape naturally following the other. Round over each grape with a flattish electric router but it is just as easily carved by hand and with a great deal more pleasure. Carve on your mark and add the date. Remove the softwood block by splitting it away with a 5/8in (15mm) No.7, taking great care not to damage the undersurface of the base. Then sand the bottom surface smooth. In order to hang the plaque securely against the wall a 1/2in (12mm) hole, 1/2in (12mm) deep, should be drilled in the centre of the back approximately 1in (25mm) down from the top edge. The top edge of the hole should be undercut with a 3/8in (9mm) No.6 to accept the head of the supporting nail.

Fig 60 The finished grapes – note how effective the simple flat outline is in framing the design.

Finishing

Sand all the easily sandable areas with reducing grades of sandpaper, being careful not to sand over crisply-carved edges. The grapes will be difficult to sand, particularly in the triangles formed where one grape meets another. This triangle is best cleaned up with a triangular punch filed up from a suitably sized nail. An alternative to sandpaper for the grapes would be to use a sanding flap-wheel fitted to an electric drill. This is a very effective method of sanding this type of carved area where edges need to be rounded over instead of crisply carved.

Very vigorously clean away all dust then seal the surface, including the bottom of the base, with varnish and sanding sealer. When the varnish is thoroughly dry, rub down with 0 grade steel wool and polish with a good quality wax polish. Use a white wax such as *Antiqwax* marble wax for the lighter-coloured woods such as chestnut which was used in this case.

THE SHAG (SCALE 2)

(Phalacrocorax aristotelis aristotelis)

The shag, green cormorant, or crested cormorant as it is variously known, differs from the European cormorant *Phalacrocorax carbo carbo* mainly in its size, which is much smaller, and also in possessing a small recurved crest in the summer. At a distance the colouring appears black but bright sunlight reveals an attractive, iridescent greenish gloss

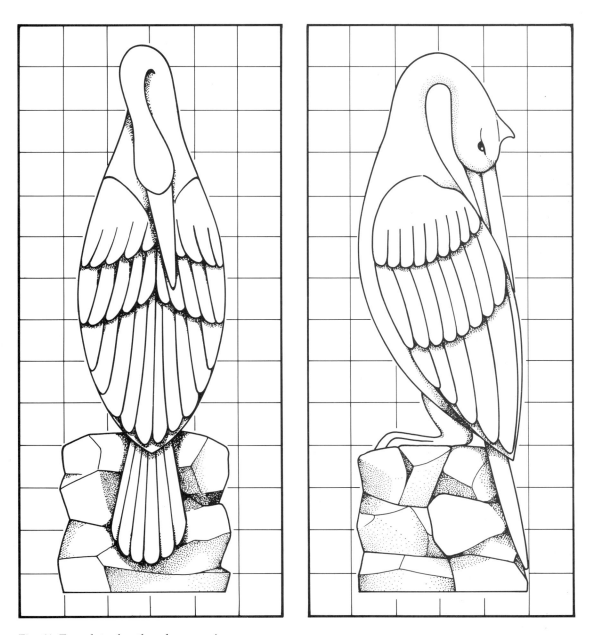

Fig 61 Template for the shag carving.

on both birds and the white face and thigh patches of the cormorant. The shag's diet consists almost exclusively of fish which it is able to out-swim, using its large webbed feet for propulsion. The larger feet are used, too, to enable the bird to rise up out of the water before diving for fish, a characteristic which also distinguishes it from the cormorant.

The pose chosen for this carving is both characteristic of the bird and right for wood. The only vulnerable sections are the beak and the tail which are firmly supported, the beak by the back and the tail by the rock. There are other equally suitable and characteristic poses that could be considered for any future shag carvings. For example, its habit of jumping out of the water before diving would make a first-class action study, or the outstretched drying wings when seated on a rock in the sun another. That particular bird pose is one of the few that enables the carver to carve a bird with outstretched wings in a reasonably sized piece of wood, due to the fact that the wings stand straight out from the body instead of at an acute angle.

Blocking In

Prepare a template from the side-view drawing, using the grid to scale it up or down to fit the available stock, and use it to mark out clearly the cleaned-up wood. Screw a square 2×2in (51×51mm) wood block to the bottom of the base to enable the work to be held in the vice (Fig 63). Remove wood from outside the lines using a 5/8in (15mm) No. 7 and carver's mallet, cleaning up the ragged outlines with a round surform.

Fig 62

Mark on the front and rear views by hand. A template cannot be used because the surface of the wood is now irregular, the side view already having been cut out. The twist in the neck is visually important and great care should be taken to ensure that it curves smoothly and gracefully from the top of the body to the back of the head. Remove wood from outside the lines with a 5/8in (15mm) No.7 and then use a 3/8in (9mm) No.10 to define the tail and to remove wood from each side of the head and neck. Note that the tail is well rounded at the tip (Fig 62).

Bosting In

Shape the carving with a 5/8in (15mm) No.7 whilst frequently consulting photographs and drawings of shags. Carry out the final shaping of the body and cleaning up with a round surform.

The Feet

Remove wood from, and roughly shape, the top surface of the rock with a 3/8in (9mm) No.6. This will allow the very large and wide webbed feet to be defined with a 3/8in (9mm) No.10. Remove wood from between the feet with a 3/16in (4.5mm) No.10. The depression between the front legs is very shallow as it is mainly concealed by the thick waterproof feathering. Carve in the depression with a 3/8in (9mm) No.6. Round over the edges of the feet and the short amount of unfeathered leg showing with a 1/4in (6mm) No.3 and carve in the two shallow depressions between the toes that indicate the webs with a 3/16in (4.5mm) No.6 (Fig 63).

The Head

Round over and shape the head, neck and beak with a 3/8in (9mm) No.3. The tip of the beak has a small hook but that is concealed by the soft feathers of the back in this pose and can be ignored. The crest, which is small, can be shaped with a medium-cut rat tail file (Fig 64).

The Eyes

The eyes lie in a long depression which can be formed with a 1/4in (6mm) No.9. This depression forms the lower edge of the rather formidable eyebrow and

Fig 63

the stop between the back of the beak and the front of the head. Form the sphere of the eyeball with a length of rod which has had a shallow depression drilled in the end as described previously and cut in a triangle at the front and rear of the eyeball with a sharp pointed craft knife. Pierce the centre of the eye with the point of a large needle to bring it to life.

Carve in the gape which runs from just forward of the eye to the tip of the bill with a 1/16in (4.5mm) No. 11

109

or by making two inclined cuts with a craft knife (Fig 64).

The Wings

A bird's wing provides lift, propulsion through the air and in some cases propulsion through the water. Its bone structure is similar to that of the human arm, wrist and hand and it is to these bones that the feathers are firmly attached.

The feathering can be roughly divided into three main groups. The long primary feathers at the wing tip which propel and steer the bird are attached to the wrist and hand bones. The secondary feathers which are smaller than the primary feathers and which provide the wing with lift and enable the bird to soar and glide. These feathers are attached to one of the forearm bones, the ulna. The smallest feathers, the wing coverts, cover the base of the large feathers and smooth the surface of the wing.

Although wing feathering is considerably more complex than this, these three main groups are the only ones normally visible and it is usually sufficient to depict only them.

Mark in the divisions between the three sets of feathers and define them with a 3/16in (4.5mm) No.10 removing the waste wood beneath each set with a 3/8in (9mm) No.3 (Fig 63). Mark in the individual feathers (Fig 64) and define them with a 1/8in (3mm) No.10, removing the wood on one side only to indicate that one feather is overlapping the next. With a 3/8in (9mm) No.3, round over the edge of the feathers with the same gouge making them almost merge into one another to give a soft, feathered look (Fig 65).

Fig 64

The Tail

The tail should be left about 3/16in (4.5mm) thick with the edges being slightly undercut, where they meet the rock, by about 1/8in (3mm). Round over the top surface of the tail and scrape clean. Mark in the tail feathers which are carved in the same way as those on the wing — there are twelve on the

110

Fig 65   The finished shag carving.

tail of the shag and fourteen on the tail of the cormorant.

The Base

Mark on all the rocks of the base in ways that naturally suggest themselves to you and define the divisions between them with a 3/8in (9mm) No.10, cutting in very deeply and repeating several times in order to get down to the required depth. Chamfer off the edges of some rocks with a 3/8in (9mm) No.3 to make them irregular in a natural way (Fig 65). Round over the edges of some

of the rocks to indicate weathering and use a suitably situated flat surface to carve your mark and add the date.

Finishing

Any of the finishes previously described would be suitable for this carving although the varnishing, rubbing down and wax polishing which produces such a lovely soft lustre on wood would probably show up the colour and grain to the best advantage.

THE BRIGANTINE (SCALE 3)

This plaque illustrates a typical, fast and sturdy brigantine of the early eighteenth century. She could have carried a reasonable amount of cargo and mounted ten cannon. This, coupled with her speed, would have enabled her crews to fight off and escape from the pirates that infested the world's oceans between about 1680 and 1730. Unfortunately this combination of speed, fire power and cargo capacity made these vessels ideal for use by the pirates themselves, and they became a prized target which, when captured, were used in turn for piracy. The crews were either forced to join the pirates or were tortured and put to death in the most terrible manner. Brigantines were extremely handsome ships and must have made a fine and exhilarating sight in a fresh wind and a choppy sea.

Blocking In

Thoroughly clean up the surface of the wood by planing or sanding and inspect

111

Fig 66 Template for the brigantine plaque.

it carefully for faults that may have to be avoided, or decorative features of the grain which may be used to indicate the sun or clouds, by careful positioning of the drawing. Screw or glue a square softwood block to the centre of the back to enable the work to be held in the vice, or use a peg board as shown on the photographs. Produce a drawing of the required size and use it to mark out the wood on the opposite side to the natural curl with carbon paper, securing the paper to the wood with Blu-Tack rather than drawing pins.

Saw out the external shape and sand the edges smooth. If a moulding is to be routed round the edge of the plaque it will need to be done before the background is lowered in order to leave a level surface for the router base to rest on. It should be routed deep enough to allow for the depth of the lowered background which is about 1/4in (6mm) deep. The edge of the plaque illustrated was formed with a beading cutter fitted with an integral guide. There are many other router cutter shapes that could have been used just as effectively, for example the ovolo, rounding over, classic, cavetto, ogee, cove. All these cutters are readily available. In addition the required moulding shape can be achieved by making two separate cuts with differently shaped cutters. Whichever cutter shapes are used, they should all be fitted with an integral guide.

Once the edge moulding has been routed out the background can be lowered with the router to a depth 1/8in (3mm) short of the moulding depth. This will leave a decorative lip round the edge of the moulding which will clearly define it (Fig 67). Clean up the edges of the design by stabbing down vertically with

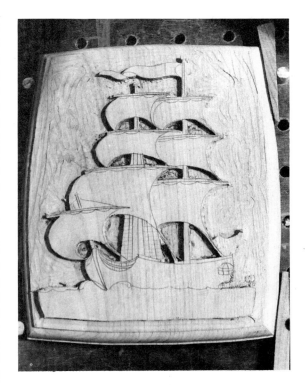

Fig 67

suitably shaped gouges.

Define the top edge of the water and the bow wave where it adjoins the hull with a 1/4in (6mm) No.9 and remove the waste wood from the bottom of the hull with a 3/8in (9mm) No.3 to round the hull over. Repeat this several times in order to get down to the required depth and to achieve a nicely rounded hull. Avoid the gallery at the stern which is left proud.

The sides and the bottom edge of the water are rounded down and merged into the background with a 5/8in (15mm) No.7. If each cut is made deeply and carefully it will satisfactorily indicate the movement of the waves.

Lower the masts where they meet the

113

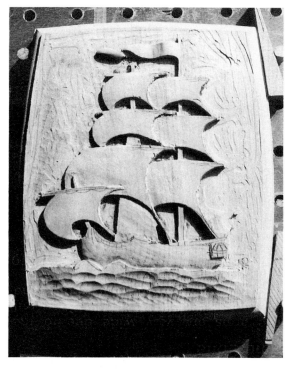

Fig 68

Fig 69

deckline by about 1/8in (3mm), tapering them nearly to the background at the tip with a 3/8in (9mm) No.3.

Define the edge of each sail where it passes behind another with a 1/4in (6mm) No.9 and remove the waste wood from the lower sail with a 3/8in (9mm) No.3. Define the bowsprit in the same way (Fig 68). Lower the tip of the mast-head flag and where it joins the mast with a 3/8in (9mm) No.3 and lower the centre of the flag almost to the background with a 3/8in (9mm) No.6. Carve in the twist in the flag with a 3/16in (4.5mm) No.9. Round over the sail edges with a 5/8in (15mm) No.3 and scrape out all the gouge marks before pencilling in the spars that are situated

at the top of each sail as shown on the top of the spritsail (Fig 69). Define all the spars with a 3/16in (4.5mm) No.9 and lower the waste wood on the sails with a 3/8in (9mm) No.3 to make the spars stand proud. Shape the flag at the stern in the same way as the mast-head flag.

The Shrouds

The shrouds are the ropes that support the masts and which have lines secured to them horizontally at close intervals to enable sailors to climb them. The shrouds on this plaque were carved in different ways. The front shrouds were raised above the surface of the background and the shrouds supporting the rear mast were incised into it. Both methods are equally effective but the incised method has the advantage that it can be used to indicate slender ropes, which would otherwise be difficult or impossible to carve, as in the case of the rope at the top of the spritsail. Carve in the front shrouds or incise them, and incise the central vertical rope and the horizontal lines with a 1/16in (1.5mm) No.11 or firmer chisel (Fig 70). The rear shrouds should be treated in the same manner.

The Hull

The gallery at the stern stands slightly proud. This is quite simply achieved by

Fig 70

rounding over the stern with a 1/4in (6mm) No.3. The square windows are small and the window frames between them are very thin so it would be difficult, if not impossible, to carve them in accurately. A simple alternative used on this plaque is to punch in the shapes of the windows lightly, with a square-ended punch which has been filed up on the flattened end of a suitably sized nail (Fig 70).

The square gun ports and the recesses between the curved rails that run from the bulkhead to the forecastle are roughly recessed with a 1/8in (3mm) No.11. The rounded corners and edges that are left are cleaned up with the pointed tip of a sharp craft knife. The bottom of the recesses can be punched with a flat-bottomed punch to even out any slight irregularities and sharpen up the edges and corners.

Incise two lines along the length of the hull above and below the gun ports with a 3/16in (4.5mm) No.11.

The recesses between the upright posts of the taffrail and the forecastle rail can be punched in in a similar fashion to that used for the gallery windows but using a smaller punch.

Mark in the stempost, narrowing it to a point where it meets the bow wave. Define each side of the stempost with a 1/8in (3mm) No.11 removing the waste wood on the hull with a 1/4in (6mm) No.3 to make the stempost stand slightly proud.

Pencil in the edge of the foam on the top of the bow wave and define it with a 1/8in (3mm) No.11, removing the waste wood below it and rounding it over with a 1/4in (6mm) No.3 (Fig 70).

Mark in the stretch creases in the sails and carve them in with a 1/4in

Fig 71 Another nautical subject finished – the highly-ornamented brigantine plaque.

(6mm) No.9 rounding over the edges and contouring them smoothly into the sails with a medium-cut rat tail file. Incise on to the spritsail the rope that runs from the top of the bowsprit to the ends of the spar (Fig 71). Indignant sailors have taken me to task for creasing their lovely wind-filled sails, so I leave you to decide whether to include the creases or not.

Thoroughly clean up the background with a scraper and reducing grades of sandpaper before incising in the seagulls in the left hand corner with either a V tool or two inclined cuts with a pointed craft knife (Fig 71). Carve your mark on the background and add the date.

Gouge a line round the edge of the plaque and approximately 3/16in (4.5mm) in from the lip to define and sharpen up the edge of the moulding clearly.

The flags are rather too small to be carved with any sort of emblem although the larger mast-head flag could quite easily be incised, perhaps with the cross of St George, using a 1/16in (1.5mm) No.11. The vertical and horizontal elements of the cross should be carefully and gently textured with the tip of a small rounded nail to make them stand out. This would give added interest to the flag which looks rather bare in my plaque.

Finishing

Relief carvings are often difficult to sand and this plaque is particularly so. It would be advisable, therefore, to restrict the type of finishing used to varnish followed by rubbing down and wax polishing. Oiled finishes would tend to darken the almost unavoidable slightly rough patches, producing an unpleasant mottled look. Great care should be taken when sanding to avoid sanding over crisply carved edges so the use of a sanding flap wheel recommended for other carvings in the book should be avoided.

THE RED SQUIRREL (SCALE 3)

This carving depicts in a typical pose the red squirrel *Sciurus vulgaris leucourus*, which is smaller, with larger tufted ears and a much bushier tail, than the imported grey squirrel *Sciurus corolinensis*. The decrease in numbers

116

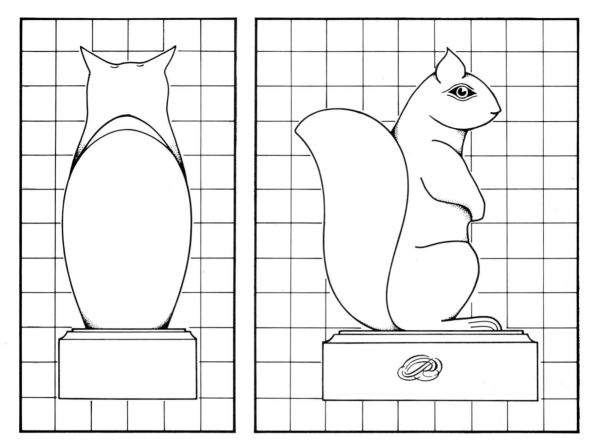

Fig 72 Template for the squirrel carving.

of the red squirrel population over recent years was once attributed to the rapid increase in the grey squirrel, but it is now thought that disease, trapping, shooting, and poisoning have been the reason for it. Soon this endearing harmless little creature that graces our countryside and which does so much good by its habit of burying surplus food and thereby distributing seeds and acorns in the forest that would otherwise die, may well, like the otter, become almost extinct.

A plain polished base with a simple decorative cove carved round the top edge was chosen to contrast sharply with the textured finish of the squirrel.

The pose, which is typical of the animal is also right for wood in that there are no vulnerable sections to be broken and the whole work can be carved from an easily obtainable sized block of wood. The carving was done in Cornish elm but the colour of teak, iroko, or Brazilian mahogany would represent the animal's colouring more faithfully and would be easier to carve and finish.

Blocking In

Produce a template from the side-view drawing and use it to mark out the cleaned-up block. Remove the wood from outside the lines with a 5/8in

117

Fig 73

Fig 74

(15mm) No.7 and carver's mallet, cleaning up the ragged outline left with a round surform.

It is quite possible to hold this work in the vice by means of its base, although it becomes difficult in the later stages when the cove has to be carved in and the base polished. It would be better to screw a 2 1/2×2 1/2in (64×64mm) wood block to the bottom of the base, as this would be much more secure and would give greater freedom.

Mark on the back and front views and remove wood from outside the lines with the 5/8in (15mm) No.7, removing all gouge marks and cleaning up with

a round surform before shaping or bosting in commences (Fig 73).

Bosting In

As with all work in the round, photographs and drawings of the subject should be obtained and consulted very frequently throughout the bosting in. That is not to say that photographs should be copied slavishly, indeed it is often necessary and desirable to stylise certain features of the carving. For example, in this carving the tail is bushier than you would normally expect in the actual animal, and the hands and arms would be held away from the body in real life and not form part of it as they do here. In both cases, however, this slight departure from realism gives the impression of much greater solidity which is so desirable in a wood carving.

Mark in the S-shaped dividing line between the tail and the body and define it very deeply with a 3/8in (9mm) No.10, removing the waste wood on each side with a 5/8in (15mm) No.3. Repeat several times in order to get down to the desired depth. Round over and shape the tail with the 5/8in (15mm) No.3 (Fig 74).

Draw on the arms and legs and define them with the 3/8in (9mm) No.10 noting that the neck is only slightly narrower than the head and that the arms cross the body to the centre where the hands hold the fir cone (Fig 75). Shape the body and head, cleaning up with a round surform.

The Head

The squirrel is a rodent, and would look very much like a rat without the large and distended cheek pouches that are such an important characteristic of its head. Great care should be taken, therefore, to get the shape of the pouches right in order to achieve a realistic head. Remove wood from between the ears with a 1/4in (6mm) No.9 using a medium-cut rat tail file for the final shaping and smoothing. The depression in the ear centre should be very shallow as it is partially concealed by the thick hair. Carve it in with a 3/16in (4.5mm) No.6.

The Eyes

The eyes of a squirrel are relatively large for a mainly diurnal animal and lie in a depression under the ears, the bottom side of the depression forming the top limit of the cheek (see Fig 75). Carve in the depression with a 3/8in (9mm) No.6, contouring the bottom edge smoothly into the cheek and the top edge into the bottom of the ear. Ensure that you have carved the depression wide enough to accommodate the large eye. Form the eyeball by stabbing down vertically with a suitably shaped gouge, say a 1/4in (6mm) No.9, and moving the gouge round in stages to complete the circle. Round over the eyeball with a 1/8in (3mm) No.3 and then cut in a triangle at the front and back corner of the eye with a sharp pointed craft knife or a 1/8in (3mm) No.3. Gouge in a shallow line right round the exterior of the eye with a 1/8in (3mm) No.10 and then pierce a small hole in the centre of the eyeball with a large needle to bring it to life. I use a large, three-cornered sailmaker's needle for this purpose.

The Nose

The nose is short and narrow, widening out rapidly to the full width of the cheek. Sand the nose with flour-grade sandpaper before cutting in the nostrils with a 1/8in (3mm) No. 10 or two inclined cuts with a craft knife (Fig 75). Due to the dense fur the mouth is not easily seen and so can safely be ignored.

The Hands, Arms, and Pine Cone

The arms are very wide due to the thickness of the fur. They slope out from the shoulders to the elbows and

Fig. 75   The squirrel carving progressing –
try to give animation to your carvings of
animals by concentrating on the features
and offering a suggestion of some character.

The Feet

Level and clean up the top surface of
the base so that the feet can be defined
with a 3/16in (4.5mm) No.10. Shape the
feet with a 1/4in (6mm) No.3 and define
the five toes with a 1/8in (1.5mm) No.10
(Fig 76).

The Base

Sand the sides of the base smooth with
reducing grades of sandpaper to obtain
a really good finish which, when
polished, will contrast sharply with the
textured surface of the squirrel. Then
carve in the cove with a 1/4in (6mm)
No.9,   smoothing   out   any   slight
irregularities left by the gouge with a
medium-cut rat tail file. Finish the cove
by sanding with flour paper wrapped
round a piece of dowel of a suitable
diameter. Alternatively, the cove, or any
other shaped moulding considered suitable, could be routed on with an electric
router.

   The sides of the base make an ideal
polished surface for your mark and the
date, which can be carved in now that
the sides of the base have been cleaned
up. The tools used to carve your mark
will vary with its complexity. A simple
monogram drawn with straight lines can
be quickly and easily incised by stabbing
down vertically with suitably sized
firmer chisels, the rounded elements of
the mark being formed with suitably
shaped gouges. I use a sharp pointed
craft knife for my monogram by making
two inclined cuts which meet in the
bottom of the V-shaped cut, the chip
then comes cleanly away.

then slope in across the body. The hands
should first be shaped with two distinct
angles, one from the wrist to the knuckles, and the other from the knuckles to
the finger tips. Define the fingers with
a 1/16in (1.5mm) No.10.

   Define the shape of the pine cone by
stabbing vertically down with a suitably
shaped gouge, say a 3/8in (9mm) No.6
and then removing the waste wood with
a 1/4in (6mm) No.3, rounding the cone
over with the same tool. Cut in the
criss-crossed lines on the fir cone with
a sharp craft knife.

Fig 76 The finished squirrel; note particularly the sharpness of the eye which contributes greatly to the effectiveness of the carving.

Texturing the Fur

The texturing to represent the fur is not strictly necessary. In fact if you have a nicely-figured piece of wood, the grain of which stands out well, it may be better to leave the surface smooth and allow the grain to suggest fur. The texturing, however, does add to the realism and if neatly carried out will not completely conceal the grain. Use a 1/8in (3mm) No.10 to make a series of cuts close together following the natural flow of the hair and allowing the gouge to run naturally out of the wood at the end of each cut to form a point. The only areas not covered by fur are the nose, eyes, feet and a very short length of leg.

Finishing

Two types of finish could be successfully used on this carving. The base can be varnished, rubbed down and wax polished repeatedly until a good soft lustre is worked up. Then the textured surface of the squirrel can be coated with two or three coats of Rustin's Danish oil at twenty-four-hour intervals. Alternatively the surface of the textured coat could be lightly sanded with flour-grade sandpaper to remove any undue roughness, and then varnished and wax polished in the same way as the base. This is the way in which the squirrel illustrated was finished.

THE HORSE'S HEAD (SCALE 3)

·The refined, elegant beauty of the horse makes it an ideal subject for the wood-carver and this particular carving is a great favourite with my students. However, not everybody agrees with my method of depicting the mane – I like to see a full mane situated fairly evenly on each side of the neck, but this is unlikely in the actual animal, where the mane is tossed more to one side of the neck than the other. I have used a little artist's licence here, but for those carvers who wish for absolute realism this point should be considered, and if it is thought necessary the drawing should be altered

121

Fig 77 The preliminary drawing shows that detail on the mane and on the features of the animal is what gives the carving its lifelike qualities.

before any carving takes place. All animals' heads can be depicted in this way; the head of one of the great shire horses in full harness is particularly handsome, or perhaps you could do the regal head of a red stag with its great curving antlers. These heads would be difficult to carve, however, and should be left until some experience with the one illustrated has been gained.

This carving was successfully carved using the base to hold the work in the vice. Soft pads were fitted to the vice jaws to prevent damage or bruising to the wood. These pads were made up from two pieces of hardboard cut to match the same shape as the jaws of the vice. They were then glued with epoxy resin to two pieces of tin plate shaped to fit over the vice jaws, so locating and holding the hardboard pads in position (see Fig 79).

The carving was worked from ash, *Fraxinus excelsior,* taken from a tree on my land that had been gale damaged. This gave it, for me, an added interest that made the extra effort required converting it and drying it properly into usable carving timber very worth while indeed. It is generally accepted that ash is a difficult carving wood but this particular piece carved crisply and finished extremely well, with the pronounced grain and the marked difference in colour between the chocolate brown heartwood and the creamy yellow of the sapwood being very effective.

Blocking In

Make up a template from the side-view drawing and use it to mark out the cleaned-up block of wood. Remove wood from outside the lines as with previous

122

carvings by using a 5/8in (15mm) No.7 and carver's mallet, cleaning up the ragged outline left with a round surform. Draw on the back and front views and remove wood from outside the lines with the 5/8in (15mm) No.7. Clean up again with the round surform, ensuring that a substantial amount of wood is left where the neck is in contact with the base for strength.

The Bosting In

The neck is oval shaped when viewed from the rear and should be left very wide during the shaping to allow enough stock for a thick mane (Fig 78). The head, when viewed from the front, has a very distinctive shape and great care should be taken to get this right. The main feature of the front view is the large depression that runs from the back of the nostril to underneath the prominent eyebrow, and the depression between the top edge of the eyebrow and the lower part of the ear. Both these depressions are best formed with a medium-cut rat tail file (Fig 80). To allow for the flared nostrils the wood should be left very wide at this point.

The Ears

A horse's ears are a beautiful and subtle shape and time taken to study photographs of them before shaping would be very well spent. The wood between the ears can be removed with a fretsaw, care being taken not to jam the blade

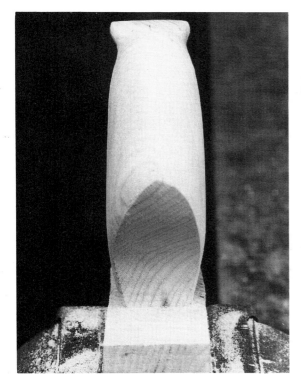

Fig 78

Fig 79

with the risk of breaking away the ear. Shape the exterior of the ear with a medium-cut rat tail file, noting that they are angled out from the head with the tips being slightly wider than the head itself. Carve in the shallow depression in the centre of the ear with a 1/8in (3mm) No.10, taking care not to over-weaken the ear which is the only vulnerable part of this carving.

The Forelock

Define the forelock with an 1/8in (3mm) No.10 removing the waste wood from each side with a 1/4 (6mm) No.3. Then make a few random cuts on the forelock with an 1/8in (3mm) No.10 following the natural curve of the hair (Fig 80).

The Eyes

The eye is well defined and expressive. Form the eyeball either with a rod with a shallow hole drilled in the end pushed firmly into the wood or by stabbing down vertically with a suitably shaped gouge and then rounding over the eyeball with a 1/8in (3mm) No.3 as has been described in previous carvings. Cut in the two triangles at the rear and front of the eyeball with a craft knife and gouge a shallow groove right round the exterior of the eye with the 1/8in (3mm) No.10. Form a small hole in the centre of the eyeball to bring it to life with a small drill rather than the point of a needle as used in previous carvings as the needle point produces too piercing a look, quite wrong for a horse's eye.

The Nostrils

Reference to photographs will show that the nostrils are situated right on the end of the nose – the tendency is to leave a small gap between the end of the nose and the nostril. This should be avoided, otherwise it will spoil the whole appearance of the head. Mark in the nostrils, ensuring that there is sufficient wood below them to carve in the mouth, and carve in the centre depression with a 1/8in (3mm) No.10 taking great care not to damage the nostril edges as they easily crumble. Remove wood from around the nostril with a 3/8in (9mm) No.7 to give the flared effect (Fig 81).

Fig 80

Fig 81 The finished horse's head; a suitably noble pose.

The Mouth

The mouth is simply defined with a 1/8in (3mm) No.10, the edges being gently rounded over with a small, fine, flat file.

The Mane

Draw on the neck the main hanks of hair and the tendrils that flow across the cheek, and define the main hanks very deeply with a 3/8in (9mm) No.10, repeating several times in order to get down to the required depth. Define the tendrils with a 1/8in (3mm) No.10 keeping the gouge cut shallow. Remove the waste wood from the neck just below the mane with a 3/8in (9mm) No.3 to make the mane stand proud from the neck.

Draw on the shallow diagonal cuts that flow smoothly across the main hanks of hair from one channel to the next and carve them in with a 1/4in (9mm) No.9. Finish the mane by making a series of small random cuts with a 1/16in (1.5mm) No.10 following the natural flow of the hair (Fig 81).

The Base

The grain and colour of the ash used for this carving was so attractive that it was decided to leave the sides of the base plain and work up a good polish to show it off to the best advantage. For less attractive woods a moulding might be considered to finish the base off in a pleasing and professional manner. The highly polished sides are an ideal surface for carving your mark and the date, which should be done at this stage.

Finishing

Unlike most carved work this carving lends itself well to a highly polished finish so great care should be taken with the sanding to get as perfect a surface as possible. The crisply-carved edges of the mane should be avoided but they could be gently rubbed down with No.1 grade steel wool to remove any slight roughness that might have been left from the gouge, without rounding over the crisply-carved edges.

After sanding rub down very vigorously with a lint-free cloth to remove all the dust and to burnish the surface of the wood. Coat with sanding sealer or varnish, and wax polish repeatedly after first rubbing down with well-worn flour paper.

THE RACING PIGEON (SCALE 3)

The wood used for this carving was Cornish elm, *Ulmus stricta,* for no other reason than that a suitable block was available. It proved, however, to be a fortunate choice as the rather wild-flecked grain showed up well on the wings and legs giving the impression of soft feathering. This was a good example of how grain can be used not only decoratively but in a practical way to indicate and emphasise a particular aspect of a carving, even if, as in this case, it was quite fortuitous.

There are many woods with a flecked grain that would be just as suitable, and two readily obtainable native hardwoods are oak and beech. It would be difficult however to carve in the final detail required round the head and legs if an

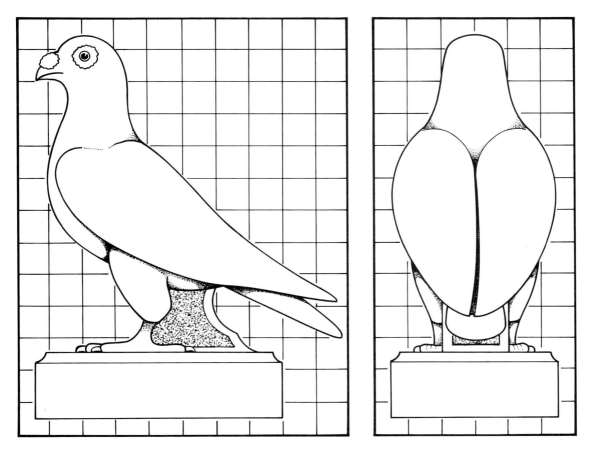

Fig 82 Template for the side and back views of the pigeon carving.

open-grained wood such as oak was used.

Any bird, when carved in the standing position illustrated, requires substantial support due to the very slender legs. Some carvers resort to the quite artificial method of securing the bird to the base with a steel rod. This practice should be avoided and a more natural method used. For example, it was arranged for the shag (Fig 65) to stand on a rock with the vulnerable legs and tail forming part of the rock and therefore strongly supported. An alternative which I often

use is to leave a shaped block of wood between the legs and the bottom of the body and the base and carve on to it suitable foliage — reeds for a water bird and perhaps bracken for a pheasant, for example. The commission for the racing pigeon, however, was to depict a particular bird and neither the rock nor the foliage would have been appropriate. In this case a shaped block of wood was left between the legs with its sides decoratively textured. This not only held the carving securely but fitted in with the simple polished base. This solution

127

is one that could well be considered for any bird carvings that you may decide to do in the future.

Blocking In

Use a template, produced from the side-view drawing, to mark out the cleaned-up wood after first inspecting the wood closely for faults. Remove wood from outside the lines with a 5/8in (15mm) No.7 and carver's mallet and clean up the ragged outlines with a round surform. Mark on the front and back views and again remove wood from outside the lines (Fig 83).

Bosting In

Shape the carving removing the bulk of the wood with a 5/8in (15mm) No.7. The wings when folded take up the shape of the body and can be safely ignored at this stage, although the general shape should be left a little oversize to allow them to be carved on later. Note that both the wattle at the base of the bill and the cere surrounding the eyes are very pronounced in the racing pigeon, and a substantial amount of wood needs to be left in these positions to allow for them (Fig 84).

Mark on the wings, including the slightly curved line down the centre of the back (Figs 83 and 84). Define the shallow back-centre line with a 3/8in (9mm) No.6 and the edge of the wings with a 3/8in (9mm) No.10. Remove the waste wood on the body below the wings with a 3/8in (9mm) No.3 leaving the wings standing well proud.

The Head

The head is not particularly difficult to carve but it does have two outstanding features which must be correct in order to achieve realism. They are the wattle at the base of the bill, which, it is believed, defects the airflow away from the pigeon's eyes during high-speed flight, and the cere surrounding the eye. They can both be seen clearly in Fig 86, but extra photographs would also be very helpful, so the head could be studied from more than one angle.

The Eye Cere and Wattle

The eye is sharp and intelligent and is completely round with no triangles at the corners. Form the eyeball with the drilled rod or by stabbing down vertically with a suitably shaped gouge as described for previous carvings. Draw on the cere defining it with a 1/8in (3mm) No.10; the edge of the cere and its top surface should be very wrinkled, with the wrinkles being lightly carved in with the 1/8in (3mm) No.10. The wattle is carved in the same way.

The Beak

The beak, particularly the tip, is very vulnerable to damage, so its final shaping is best carried out with thin strips of fine sandpaper pulled back and forth between the hands. This method will also allow the beak to be brought to a fine point. Stick masking tape to the back of the sanding strips to prevent them breaking. Cut in the gape with a sharp pointed craft knife, rather than attempting it with a small gouge, which will only result in damage to the beak tip.

Fig 83

Fig 84

The Wings

Mark on the long steering and propelling primary feathers and slightly reduce their height at the point where they are overlapped by the smaller secondary feathers. The secondaries in their turn are overlapped by the wing coverts, but on the softly feathered wing of the pigeon this junction is barely perceptible and can be safely ignored. It is sufficient to reduce the size of the feathers progressively. Define each feather with a 1/8in (3mm) No.10, making very shallow cuts, and then remove the waste wood from one side of the cut only. This will indicate that one feather overlaps its neighbour. Produce the soft feathered look by carefully filing with a small, fine, flat file all the edges of the feathers and then sand them until the edges almost fade into the background (Fig 86). The feathering carved on the wing adds very considerably to the realism but it is not absolutely necessary and it may be found desirable to omit it altogether if a nicely-figured wood has been used.

The Legs and Feet

The legs are feathered throughout most of their length, the short unfeathered length remaining and the feet being covered with scales. It is now believed that the scales are some evidence that birds in the past have evolved from reptiles. The feet have four toes, three facing forwards and one facing backwards, each toe culminating in a small claw.

129

Fig 85

Shape the leg before drawing on the feet and then define the four toes with a 1/8in (3mm) No.10, removing the waste wood from around them with a 3/16in (4.5mm) No.6. Continue with the same gouge to level and texture the top surface of the base (Fig 85). Round over the toes and the legs with a 1/4in (6mm) No.3 using fine-grade sandpaper for the final shaping and cleaning up. Bring the claws to a sharp edge with a small, flat, fine file and make a series of shallow cuts across the feet and the bottom part of the leg with a 1/16in (1.5mm) No.10 to indicate the scales (Fig 85).

The Supporting Block

Finish shaping and cleaning up the supporting block and pencil in a line 3/16in (4.5mm) from its edge. Define the line with a 1/8in (3mm) No.10. This will give a clear-cut dividing line between the texturing and the edge of the block. Texture the surface between the gouged lines by tapping in a nail at close intervals that has had its point rounded over with a file or by grinding on a stone

The Base

Clean up the sides of the base by sanding and then, if desired, carve a cove round the top edge with a 1/4in (6mm) No.9. Clean the cove up with a rat tail file and finish with a piece of fine sandpaper wrapped round a length of dowel of a suitable diameter. It may be felt that a moulding routed round the top edge of the base would be more attractive than the carved cove, but, as is often the case with carved work, some part of the carving overhangs the base, in this case the tail, making it impossible for

Fig 86 The familiar figure of the racing pigeon given a proud stance and a certain nobility.

131

the router base to pass. Carve on the base side your mark and add the date.

Finishing

The carving illustrated was varnished, rubbed down and then worked up to a lovely soft lustre with a good quality wax polish. Any of the finishes described in the chapter on finishing would be suitable though.

THE NORTH AMERICAN BISON (SCALE 4)

The North American Bison, *Bison bison,* is larger and generally more massively built than its European cousin *Bison bonasus,* the large bulls often exceeding one and a half tons in weight. This enormous size and strength often leads to serious injury or even death during the summer breeding season when the great bulls compete for the favour of the cows.

It has been estimated that in the region of one hundred million bison once roamed freely over the vast open plains of North America, but the introduction of modern weapons and colonisation led to an indiscriminate slaughter which at the end of the last century almost brought them to extinction. With careful breeding and protection in law their numbers have recovered to about thirty thousand animals in the wild, and they are now controlled at about this figure. It is immensely satisfying that in this case man has acted just in time to save the complete extinction of this regal animal.

The massive outlines and sheer bulk of the bison are so dramatic and impressive that it is sufficient to choose a static pose such as the one illustrated (which, incidentally, is also a typical stance of the animal), in order to depict it in an interesting and natural way. Other alternative poses which might be considered, once experience has been gained with this carving, would be a fight between two of the big bulls or a charging bull, which would be an exciting action study, or perhaps (when considerable experience has been gained) a complete bison family.

The wood used for the carving illustrated was English elm. Any hardwood would be suitable but a rich brown iroko or (if you are very rich) teak, would not only carve well but would also indicate the colouring of the animal's coat in a natural way.

Blocking In

Use the grid on the side-view drawing to produce a template which can then be used to mark out the cleaned-up wood. Remove wood from outside the lines, either with a bandsaw or by sawing radially at close intervals and then splitting the wood away with a 5/8in (15mm) No.7 and carver's mallet. Clean up the rough surface with a round surform. Screw a block of wood approximately 2 1/2×2 1/2in (64×64mm) square to the bottom of the base to enable the work to be held securely in the vice.

Remove wood you can see between the legs when looking from the side, leaving the wood seen between the legs when looking from the back or front for strength, to be removed later when the heavy bosting in has been completed.

The wood can be removed from in between the legs either with a jigsaw after drilling in a suitable sized hole to take the jigsaw blade, or by first drilling the bulk of wood away and then removing the remainder with a 3/8in (9mm) No.10. Ensure that sufficient wood is left for the sheath and testes as they can be easily overlooked at this stage. Remove wood from each side of the tail and block it in with a 1/4in (6mm) No.9 and a 1/4in (6mm) No.3.

Draw on the back and front views by hand and remove wood from outside the lines with a 5/8in (15mm) No.7,

leaving the horns the full width of the block. Clean up with a round surform (Fig 89).

The head, which is very massive, is covered with thick dense hair, as are the shoulders. This dense hair extends back approximately halfway along the body, and there is a clear-cut dividing line between the shoulder hair and the almost hairless rear half of the body. Mark in the dividing lines between the head and the shoulders and the front and rear half of the body, and define them very deeply with a 3/8in (9mm) No.10. Repeat several times in order to

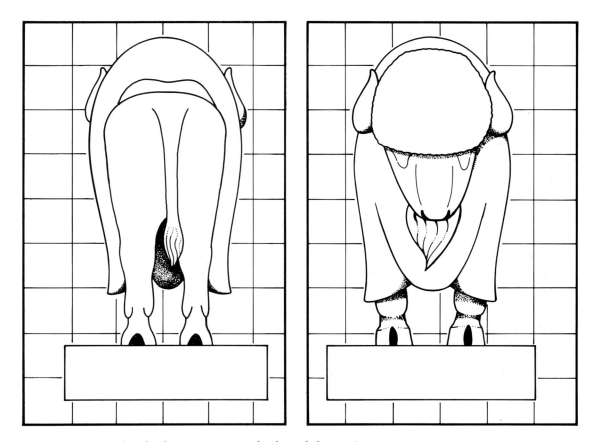

Fig 87 Template for the bison carving – back and front views.

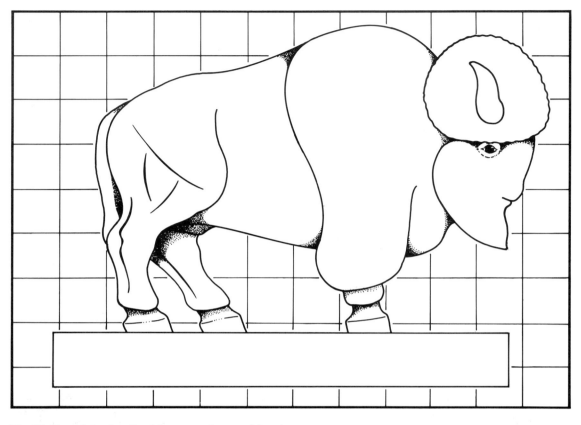

Fig 88 Template for the bison carving – side view.

get down to the required depth. Reduce the width of the rear half of the body and the flanks with the 5/8in (15mm) No.7, leaving the shoulders approximately 3/8in (9mm) wider (Fig 89).

Produce a template of the horn and use it to mark out the horns on each side of the head ensuring that they are symmetrical. Draw a square round the horn positions and remove wood from outside the lines with a 3/8in (9mm) No.10 leaving a square block in the horn position (Fig 89).

Bosting In

Carefully study photographs of bison both before and at frequent intervals during the bosting in. Remove the bulk of the wood with a 5/8in (15mm) No.7, using a much flatter gouge, say a 5/8in (15mm) No.3, to round off the edges and remove most of the gouge marks. Clean it all up with a round surform noting that the flanks have a powerful flattish look and are not very rounded (Fig 90).

The Head

Use a medium-cut rat tail file to clean up the whole head carefully before starting on the detail.

134

Fig 89

Fig 90

135

The Horns

The horns are inward-curved and very robust. They stand proud of the head, of course, but the curly hair surrounding them is so thick and dense that in some animals they appear to be part of the head. It is sufficient, therefore, only to undercut the horns slightly, leaving them solidly attached to the head throughout their length, and only freeing the tip, if so desired, for realism. Use the horn template to mark out the horns clearly on the two blocks of wood previously left on each side of the head, taking great care to get them symmetrical. Block in the horns by stabbing down vertically with gouges that fit the horn contours, say a 3/8in (9mm) No.6 and a 1/4in (6mm) No.3 (Fig 90). Shape the horns by rounding them over with a 3/8in (9mm) No.3 using a rat tail file for the final shaping and cleaning up. Carve a small, shallow channel round the bottom of the horn where it enters the head to indicate where the hair is indented by the horn (Fig 91).

The Eyes

The eyes lie in a small hairless triangle situated just below the front of the horn and appear to be small in relation to the great bulk of the massive head. Mark in the triangle and define it with a 1/8in (3mm) No.10, recessing it to the depth of about 1/8in (3mm) with a 1/8in (3mm) No.3 and rounding the edges of the triangle with the same tool.

Ensure that the bottom of the recess is flat and properly cleaned up before putting in the eye. An eye as small as this would be difficult to carve by stabbing down vertically as described for previous carvings, so it would probably be better to use a length of rod with a shallow sphere drilled in the end pushed firmly into the wood. This was the method used for the carving illustrated. Drill a small hole in the centre of the eyeball to create the shadow that will bring the eye to life.

The Nose

The nose is broad and flat and the nostrils are simply carved in with a very small quick gouge using a 1/16in (1.5mm) No.11, or by two inclined cuts with a sharp craft knife.

The Beard

The beard is a distinctive and important feature of the head and is long and shaggy. Mark in the main hanks of hair (Fig 91) and define them with a 1/4in (6mm) No.9. Make a series of random cuts with a 1/8in (3mm) No. 10 following the natural flow of the hair (Fig 92).

The Legs

The front legs are covered by a mass of long shaggy hair which extends nearly down to the hoof, and the rear legs are completely devoid of hair. Remove the wood that was left for strength between the front and rear legs after first ensuring that the external shape of the legs is absolutely right. It is a common fault here to remove wood from between the legs only to find more needs to be taken off the external shape later so leaving them too narrow. Ensure that sufficient wood is left between the rear legs to carve in the sheath and testes.

The long shaggy hair covering the

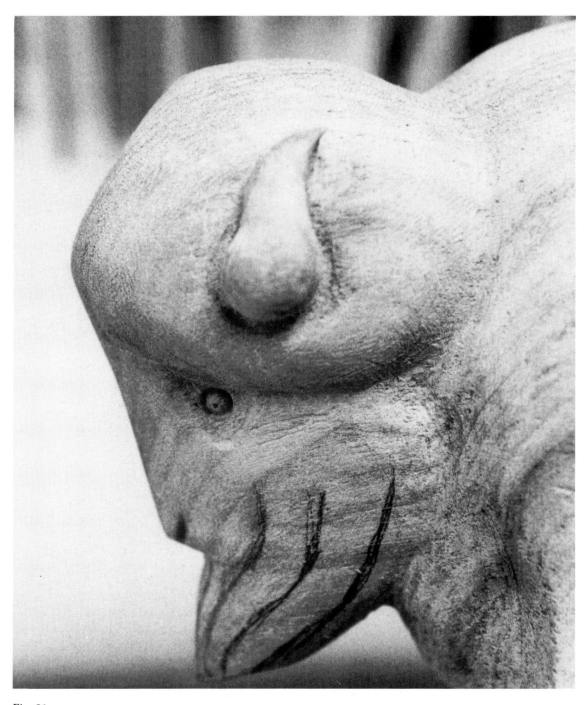

Fig 91

Fig 92 The bison; here it is power and strength that are highlighted.

lower half of the front legs is carved in the same manner as that used to carve the beard. The top surface of the base needs to be levelled in order that the hooves can be shaped. Level the top surface carefully, keeping the gouge cuts even, as these gouge marks will be left in the top surface when the base is finished.

Use a flat file to finish rounding the hooves and cut in the V of the cleft hoof with a 3/8in (9mm) 60° V tool, or by making two inclined cuts with a 3/8in (9mm) No.3. The recess behind the hoof is formed by stabbing down vertically with a 1/4in (6mm) No.9 removing the chip with a 1/8in (3mm) No.3 (Fig 92).

Mark on the muscles on the rear leg and define them with a 1/4in (6mm) No.9 rounding off the edges with a 1/4in (6mm) No.3. Contour them smoothly into the legs with a suitably shaped riffler file. The dew claws are situated at the bottom of the rear leg, the shallow channel between them being carved in with a 1/8in (3mm) No. 10.

The Tail

The tail is thin and should be left attached to the right rear leg for strength. The hairs of the tuft at the end of the tail can be indicated with a few random cuts with a 1/16in (1.5mm) No.10. Now shape the sheath and testes, the bulk of waste wood being removed with riffler files due to the inaccessibility (Fig 92).

The Base

The completely plain base harmonises well with this carving, although an irregularly shaped base with fissures and protruding rocks would be appropriate and might well be considered in order to make the carving an individual one. Don't forget your mark and the date.

Finishing

All the finishes mentioned in the chapter on finishing would be suitable for this carving, although it would not look well with a high gloss finish. The work illustrated was varnished and wax polished, the wax being finally rubbed down gently with 00 grade steel wool to remove any gloss.

THE POINTER (SCALE 4)

The origins of this handsome aristocratic sporting dog are unknown, although it is believed to have been in existence in its present form for about eighty years. The head is particularly well formed and handsome and is characterised by a nose that is slightly turned up at the tip, the tip being above the horizontal line of the muzzle. Affectionate, intelligent and obedient, the pointer makes an ideal companion in the field where its long muscular body gives it an untiring performance. When game is detected the dog assumes the motionless, statuesque stance from which it derives its name. This characteristic pose was chosen for the carving, not only because it is dramatic in itself, but also because the pricked-up ears, outstretched neck and tail, and the general stance unmistakeably show the dog's tense, nervous excitement.

The need to illustrate motion or character in a solid block of wood is a problem that often confronts the carver and there is often a conflict between the appearance of an animal and its general character. For example the great Shire horses, with their masses of bulging muscle, give the impression of a danger and ferocity which is quite out of keeping with the gentle, obedient loyalty which is their most endearing characteristic. So the pose chosen to depict any animal should, as far as is practically possible, reflect not only its appearance but also its character.

The legs in this carving are particularly vulnerable to damage but this is reduced by allowing two of the legs to sink into the surrounding grass which in turn gives some support. An alternative would be to leave wood between the belly and the base and then carve on to it appropriate foliage such as bracken, but this would tend to detract from the clean line of the carving and reduce the visual impact.

A softwood block, glued in position between the raised front leg and the base after the carving has been blocked in, gives support during the carving. The block is easily cut away at the end.

The Wood

The wood used was an unusually straight-grained piece of Cornish elm, *Ulmus stricta*, its sinewy strength making it ideal for supporting the slender legs. More fragile woods, such as most of the mahoganies, should be avoided where possible. The flecked nature of

139

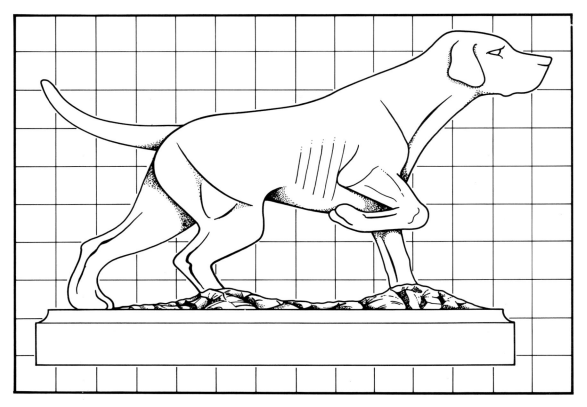

Fig 93 Template for the pointer carving.

the grain, which on the pigeon carving was used to depict the soft feathering, can be seen clearly on the side of the base (Fig 99).

Blocking In

The base of this carving could be used to hold the works in the vice but it would be much more secure and easier to work if a 2 1/2in (64mm) square block was screwed to the bottom of the base to enable the work to be held securely.

Produce the template from the side-view drawing and use it to mark out the wood. Remove wood from outside the lines with a 5/8in (15mm) No.7 and clean up the ragged outlines with a round surform. Mark on the front and back views and remove wood from outside the lines, again cleaning up with the round surform. Ensure during this stage of the carving that all surfaces are kept flat with no attempt being made to round over edges or shape the carving. Remove wood seen between the legs from the side, leaving wood seen between the back legs when looking from the back or front, to maintain strength whilst the carving proceeds. Note that the top surface of the base is left about 1/4in (6mm) too thick to allow for the carving of the grass at a later stage. If required, you can glue a softwood block in between the raised front leg and the base to support the work during the carving.

140

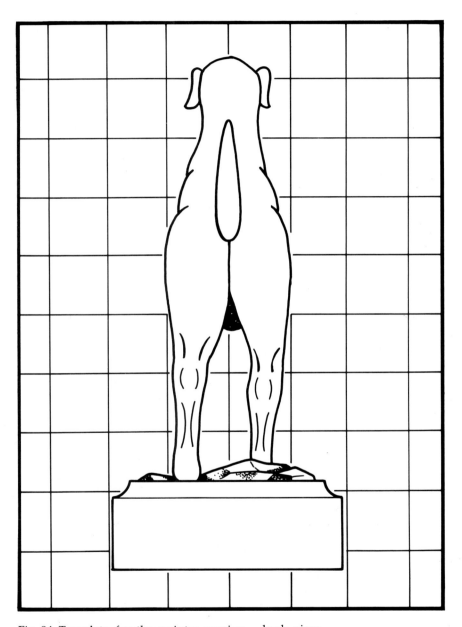

Fig 94 Template for the pointer carving – back view.

Fig 95

Fig 96

142

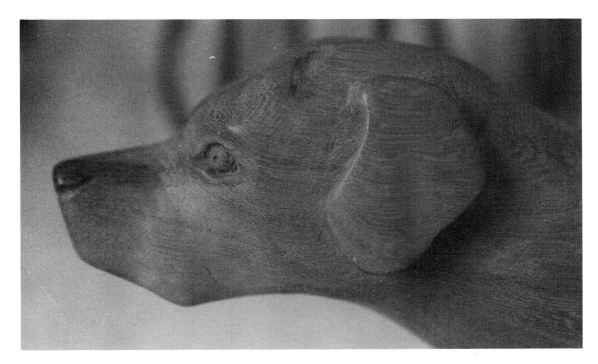

Fig 97

Bosting In

To enable the rear left paw and the two legs where they enter the grass to be shaped, the top edge of the base should now be levelled, preferably with a router, and the top surface carved roughly to its finished shape.

The lean, lithe shape of the pointer is a particularly subtle one and it will be necessary to consult photographs at very frequent intervals during the bosting in to get it right.

Bost in or shape the carving with a 5/8in (15mm) No.7 and carver's mallet, using a round surform for the final shaping. Thoroughly clean up the whole surface with a rat tail file and scrape out any rough patches with a carver's scraper before the final phase, the carving of the detail, commences (Fig 96).

The Head

The head is well formed, with a prominent bone structure which gives it a very attractive angularity. Note the slightly upturned nose, the swelling of the jowls at the back of the mouth, and the pricked-up ears.

The Ears

Block in the ears by first producing a template from the side view drawing. This will enable identical ears to be drawn on each side of the head. Use the template to mark out the ears, ensuring that they are symmetrical before stabbing down vertically with gouges whose sweeps fit the ear contours.

Shape the ears as shown in Fig 97 and undercut the front and the bottom half of the ears with a shallow cut using a 1/8in (3mm) No.10.

The Eyes

Form the sphere of the eyeball either with a length of rod which has had a shallow hole drilled in the end and which is then pushed firmly into the wood, or by stabbing down vertically with a suitably shaped gouge which is moved round in stages until the sphere is complete, and then round over with a 1/8in (3mm) No.3. Cut a triangle in at the front and rear corner of the eye with a sharp pointed craft knife, and gouge a shallow channel round the exterior of the eye rounding over its edges with a fine file (Fig 97). Pierce a small hole in the centre of the eyeball with a large needle to bring it to life.

The Nostrils and Mouth

Use a 1/16in (1.5mm) No.10 or two inclined cuts with a craft knife to cut in the nostril and then gouge in the mouth with a 1/8in (3mm) No.11. The mouth runs underneath the jowls from the front of the muzzle to the swellings which are formed at the back of the mouth when it is closed (Fig 97).

The Neck, Ribs and Tail

Carve in the shallow depression which runs from the back of the head almost to the chest in the lower half of the neck with a 3/8in (9mm) No.6 and then contour the edges smoothly into the neck with a medium-cut rat tail file and scraper. Round off the tail with files, finishing with strips of sandpaper pulled back and forth between the two hands, noting that it gets thinner towards the tip.

On a dog in first-class condition the ribs are only just visible on the chest cage but it will be difficult to make a sufficiently shallow cut with a carving gouge, although it is possible. An easier alternative is to file in the slight depressions between the ribs with a fine rat tail file, carefully rounding over the tops of the depressions so formed with the same file. Remember that when the carving is polished they will be very much more visible. The depth of cut required can be judged from Fig 99.

The Legs

The legs are shapely and muscular, the muscles, particularly in this tense pose, being very prominent, as is the bone

Fig 98

Fig 99 The finished pointer dog, limbs taut, ready to spring.

structure. Mark in all the muscles and define them with a 1/4in (6mm) No.9, removing the waste wood with a 1/4in (6mm) No.3. Contour the muscles smoothly into the legs with a fine rat tail file, and small scrapers made up from strips hacksawed off a cabinet scraper with the ends ground to the required contour (Fig 98). Note that the front raised leg is left attached to the chest cage throughout its length for strength. Remove the wood that was left between the rear legs for strength and shape the testes and sheath with a riffler file.

File the one visible paw into a ball shape and then with a rat tail file of a suitable diameter, say a 1/4in (6mm), file a shallow depression round the front of the paw and about halfway up. This depression can just be seen in Fig 99. Make the three cuts that divide the toes with a 1/8in (3mm) No.11, and remove the softwood block from between the

upraised leg and the base if one has been fitted.

The Base

Carve a series of deep gouge cuts over the top surface of the base with a 5/8in (15mm) No.7 ensuring that each one forms a deep smooth depression. It will help in achieving a smooth surface if the cutting edge of the gouge is moved sideways as it is pushed into the wood, so providing a slicing cut. Make a series of cuts with a small V tool on the surface of each depression, all radiating from the same point, to indicate that the dog is standing on grass or reedy ground (Figs 98 and 99). Carve a cove round the top edge of the base with a 1/4in (6mm) No.9 smoothing it with a rat tail file and sandpaper wrapped round a short length of dowel of a suitable diameter. Carve on the side of the base your mark and the date.

Finishing

The carving illustrated was varnished, rubbed down and then wax polished. Any of the finishes mentioned in the chapter on finishes would, however, be suitable.

THE BLACK RHINOCEROS (SCALE 4)

The black Rhinoceros *(Diceros bicornis)* is smaller than the white Rhinoceros *Ceratotherium,* and has a proportionately smaller head and smaller ears. The upper lip is triangular in shape, flexible, and prehensile. This serves to identify it from the white Rhinoceros which has a wide, square, upper lip and a large hump at the base of the neck. The statistics of this magnificent creature are almost beyond belief. It is about 12ft (4m) long, stands 5ft (1.5m) high at the shoulder, with large males weighing in in excess of 2 tons (over 2 tonnes). It is entirely vegetarian, feeding on leaves, acacia bark and shoots, which it wrenches off with its prehensile upper lip. Although it is more unpredictable than the white Rhinoceros and extremely dangerous when provoked, it normally poses no threat to man and will continue to browse peacefully unless approached too closely. It has been estimated that about twenty thousand black Rhinoceroses once roamed freely over the open savannas of central Africa. These numbers have been reduced, mainly during the 1970's and 1980's, to about five hundred, with thousands being massacred by poachers for their horns, believed to contain

Fig 100 Template for the rhinoceros carving – side view.

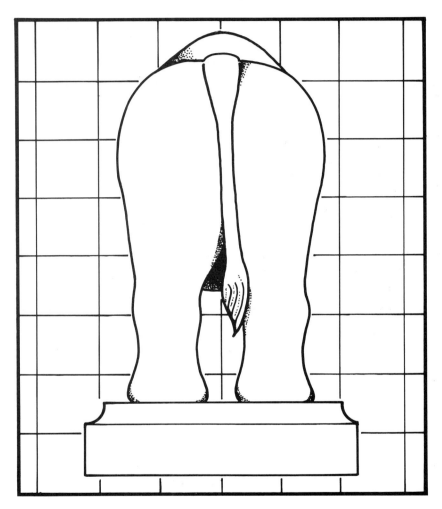

Fig 101 Template for the rhinoceros carving – back view.

aphrodisiac qualities. More recently the elaborately carved Djambia dagger, which is considered to be a status symbol in the Middle East and which has a rhinoceros horn handle, has been the cause of this senseless slaughter. Fortunately the Kenyan government, with great far-sightedness, is now providing sanctuaries where the animals can be protected and live in reasonable safety, and where their numbers may eventually increase until they are no longer in danger of extinction. This work is being greatly assisted by the Rhino Rescue Trust, a charitable body in Britain, which endeavours to raise the considerable amount of money required to carry out this work.

I have stressed the need in previous chapters to obtain and study with great care photographs and pictures of the animals or birds being carved. This is particularly important with the rhinoceros whose massive balanced beauty cannot be fully understood or appreciated without such careful study. Indeed it will be found that the work will be nearly finished before a complete understanding is achieved. It is this new vision and understanding of the wonderful creatures around us that makes the carver's world so much more exciting and visually rewarding.

The Wood

The wood used for this carving was Cornish elm, *Ulmus stricta*, its sinewy strength making possible the cross-grain carving of the slender horn. Any hardwood would be suitable for this carving, although if a less tough and sinewy wood was used it would be advisable to point the horn more forward in line with the direction of the grain. This would still be realistic, as some individual animals do have the horn pointing straight ahead instead of nearly vertical as illustrated in the carving.

The pose chosen for this carving is a characteristic one, the rhinoceros being seen more often than not in this stance despite its reputation. Once experience has been gained with this carving, however, perhaps a grazing rhinoceros surrounded by cattle egrets, or a charging rhinoceros with its head lowered and tail erect would make pleasing and exciting studies.

Blocking In

Screw a 2 1/2in (64mm) square wood block to the bottom of the base to enable the work to be held securely in the vice then use the grid on the side-view drawing to produce a template that will fit the available wood. Mark out the block and remove wood from outside the lines with a 5/8in (15mm) No.7 and carver's mallet or, if available, a bandsaw. Draw on the back and front views and remove wood from outside the lines, noting that the belly is much wider than either the shoulders or the flanks, and that the head, because of the width of the ears, is as wide as the shoulders. Remove wood seen between the legs from the side, leaving the wood seen between the legs when looking from the back or front, until it is decided that the external shape of the legs is absolutely correct. Remove the waste wood with a jigsaw or by drilling the bulk of wood away, then removing the rest with a 3/8in (9mm) No.10. The tail is supported throughout its length by the extended

Fig 102

right rear leg. Remove wood from each side of the tail with a 3/8in (9mm) No.10, leaving it over-wide at this stage, until the exact position of the inside of the right rear leg has been established. Remove the unwanted legs on each side of the carving with a 5/8in (15mm) No.10 and clean up the whole work with a round surform (Fig 102).

Bosting In

Bost in the body with a 5/8in (15mm) No.7 and when the external shape of the rear legs has been accurately established, remove the wood that was left between them with a 3/8in (9mm) No.10. The tail can now be reduced to its final shape and bosted in. Note that the tail is thin with a small tuft at the end (Fig 105) and that there is a pronounced roll of hide at the top of the front legs. Clean up the carving with a round surform (Fig 103).

The Head

The head seems to be small in relation to the massive body but it is much wider than it appears at first sight. It is a wise precaution, therefore, to leave the head a little wider than is at first considered necessary, reducing it as the shaping takes place and the correct width becomes more evident.

The Ears

The ears are more on the side of the head and smaller than those of the

149

Fig 103

white rhinoceros, the edges often being frayed and torn. Remove the waste wood from between the ears with a fretsaw, taking care not to allow the blade to jam and impose a load on the ear which might break it off. Shape the ears with files rather than carving gouges and note that they are angled outwards slightly instead of facing straight ahead. Carve a shallow depression in the centre of the ear with a 3/16in (4.5mm) No.6 and if so desired produce the ragged torn look on the ear edges with a small V tool or sharp craft knife. Bost in the whole head and shape and finish the horns with files and strips of sandpaper. Fix sticky tape or masking tape to the back of the strips of sandpaper to prevent them breaking. Note that there is a large bulge at the base of each horn and above the eye which must be taken into account when bosting in the head (Fig 104).

The Eyes

The eyes are small and surrounded by deep wrinkles. Produce the eyeball with a length of drilled rod which has had a shallow sphere drilled in the end (as has been described for previous carvings). Carve in the pronounced wrinkles beneath it with a 1/8in (3mm) No.10 rounding over the tops with a small rat tail file.

The Nostrils

The nostrils are situated right at the front of the head and are oval-shaped.

150

Fig 104

Mark them in taking great care to see that they are symmetrical when viewed from the front, and then carve in the central depression with a 1/4in (6mm) No.9. Remove wood from round the exterior edge of the nostril with the same tool, smoothing it into the head with a rat tail file, so leaving the nostril standing proud (Fig 104).

The Mouth

Carve in the mouth with a 1/8in (3mm) No.10, noting that the upper lip over-hangs the lower by a considerable extent and that the mouth is only just visible. The front of the head is extensively wrinkled, carve in the wrinkles with a 1/8in (3mm) No.10, smoothing over the top edges with a small rat tail file (Fig 104).

The Neck

The thick hide of the neck causes deep rounded furrows to form when the head is raised or lowered. Cut in these furrows very deeply with a 3/16in (4.5mm) No.10, rounding over the tops and contouring them smoothly into the neck with a rat tail file (Figs 104 and 106).

The Body

The backbone is visible and very prom-inent from just rear of the shoulder to

151

where it joins the tail. Remove wood from each side of the backbone with a 1/4in (6mm) No.9 and a 1/4in (6mm) No.3, leaving the backbone about 3/16in (4.5mm) wide, and if absolute realism is required the very slight depressions between the vertebra can be filed in with a small rat tail file to give a knobbly appearance.

Rather surprisingly for such a large animal the ribs show up distinctly, although they are in fact quite shallow. There are usually seven visible and they should be filed in with a rat tail file which will also round over the tops of the depressions. Use as fine a file as can be obtained because, although it will take a little longer, it will leave a much cleaner depression which would otherwise be difficult to clean up (Fig 106).

The Shoulders, Front Legs and Toes

The shoulders have two shallow depressions running across them caused by the wrinkling of the thick hide. The position of each depression is dependent on the position of the leg. Carve in the depressions with a 3/8in (9mm) No.6, smoothing them over and contouring them into the shoulders with a rat tail file and small scraper. Round over the prominent fold of hide at the top of each front leg with a 1/4in (6mm) No.3 and a flat file (Fig 106).

The front of the foot is divided into three toes, each with a prominent toe nail. The depression between each toe is carved in with a 3/16in (4.5mm) No.6. This depression runs from the bottom of the foot to nearly halfway up the leg, and it should be smoothed into the

Fig 105

leg with files. The toe nail is first defined by stabbing down vertically with a gouge whose sweep matches the shape of the toe nail. The wood at the edges of the cut so formed is then removed with a 1/8in (3mm) No.3 (Fig 106).

The Rear Legs

There is a thick fold of hide at the forward edge of each flank. Undercut the flank, leading edge first, with a 3/16in (4.5mm) No.10 followed by a 1/8in (3mm) No.10 to achieve greater depth, taking care not to crumble the leading edge of the flank. Reduce the wood

Fig 106   The more exotic figure of the rhinoceros is here seen in all its glory.

behind the leading edge with a 3/8in (9mm) No.6 using files to smooth this depression into the flank and to round over its leading edge. A further depression across the flank just to the rear of the one just carved can be clearly seen in Fig 106. The rear toes are carved in the same way as the front.

The Base

The simple polished base used for this carving was intended to complement the massive dramatic beauty of this magnificent animal to the best advantage. For those carvers wishing to make their carving realistic and unique, however, an irregularly shaped base with some form of foliage either incised or carved on it (similar to that used for the pointer)

would look just as good. Carve a cove round the top edge of the base with a 1/4in (6mm) No.9, smoothing it with a rat tail file. Sadly the finished carving will depict an animal that may soon no longer exist on this earth, so that it is of even greater importance than usual that your mark and the date are carved on the base side.

Finishing

This carving was wax polished after the preliminary varnishing and rubbing down. I have felt since, however, that it would have looked particularly well oiled with Rustin's Danish oil or similar finish, but this is a matter of opinion, so I will leave you to decide on the finish to use.

THE GALLOPING SHIRE STALLION (SCALE 4)

The 'great horse of England', as the Shire was once known, is the largest and heaviest of the draught horses bred in this country. Its enormous strength makes it particularly popular for agricultural work, where it is quite capable of drawing a five-ton load with ease. By character it is docile, loyal and obedient with a very deep bond of affection often being built up between horse and master. The predominant colours are bays and browns, usually accompanied by a good deal of white on the legs and feathering.

There are many suitable hardwoods available that would give a choice of colours to add realism to the work, but it would be of particular interest if one were chosen which had a marked difference in colour between the heartwood and the sapwood. A good example is yew, where the sapwood is a light creamy yellow and the heartwood either reddish or a rich brown. It would not be difficult to block in the carving in such a way that the creamy yellow heartwood was positioned at the bottom of the legs and the feathering, giving them a realistic whitish appearance. I

Fig 107 Template for the carving of the galloping Shire horse.

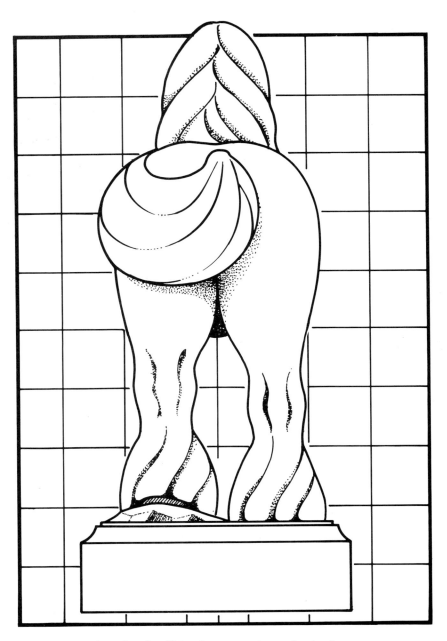

Fig 108 Template for the Shire horse carving – back view.

have used this method in the past to provide an interesting contrasting colour for a horse's mane or tail and have found it to be very effective indeed. With a little careful thought, when wood is being selected for a particular carving, the beautiful colours and grain can be used by the carver to enhance the work in a subtle and natural way.

Blocking In

Firmly screw a 2 1/2×2 1/2×4in (64×64×102mm) wood block to the bottom of the base to enable the work to be held securely in the vice. As there is a good deal of heavy bosting in to be done on this carving it would be advisable to make up a strong canvas bag about 18in (457mm) square and partially fill it with a mixture of dry sand and sawdust. This will hold and support the work overall when the carving is bedded down into it and the heavy bosting in is being carried out.

Produce a template from the side-view drawing and position it on the wood in a way that will make the best use of the grain and colour. It would greatly increase the strength of the legs if the grain were arranged to run vertically up them, but this would inevitably mean that the top surface of the horse would be end grain which is particularly difficult to clean and polish up. There is, however, sufficient strength in the sturdy legs to make this unnecessary if the carving is large enough.

Use the template to mark out the wood and remove wood from outside the lines, either with a bandsaw or by sawing in radially at close intervals. Then split the wood away with a 5/8in (15mm) No.7 and carver's mallet. Clean

Fig 109

up the rough surface with a round surform. Remove wood seen between the legs from the side view with a jigsaw, if one is available, or by first drilling the bulk of the wood away and removing the rest with a 3/8in (9mm) No.10. Remove the unwanted wood on the legs each side being careful not to overlook the sheath. Remove wood seen between the legs when looking from the back or front once the external shape of the legs has been accurately determined.

The raised front hoof will require some support during the carving, and it can be glued in a softwood wedge between the raised leg and the top of the base, to be removed later when the work is complete. An alternative that might be

Fig 110

Bosting In

considered would be to make the top surface of the base much more irregular and support of the leg in this way, rather in the way that the rear left leg is supported. Although this would be stronger it would tend to look artificial. Draw on the back and front views noting that the belly is wider than either the chest or flanks, and that the tail where it crosses the flanks is the full width of the wood (Fig 109).

Partially block in the tail, leaving the final blocking in until the flanks have been bosted in and their final shape, where the tail crosses them, has been accurately established.

To enable the hooves to be shaped, the irregular top surface of the base should be carved roughly to its final shape after first levelling the edge, preferably with a router. Whilst the router is in use it will be convenient to rout in the cove round the top edge or, if preferred, a moulding.

Shape the whole carving with a 5/8in (15mm) No.7, consulting photographs and pictures of Shires throughout. The sandbag can be used to advantage during this phase in order to absorb the heavy blows required and to save the legs from undue stress. Complete the blocking in of the tail when the flanks have

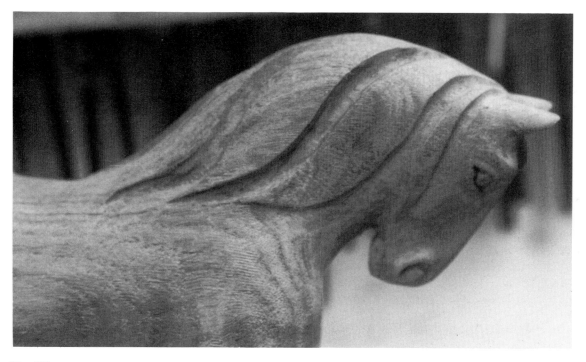

Fig 111

been shaped and then bost it in. Note that the neck and the feathering has been left very wide so that it can be carved deeply later (Fig 110).

The Head and Ears

The ears are long, sharp and sensitive, their shape being very subtle. They have an important effect on the appearance of the whole head. Remove wood from between the ears, preferably with a fretsaw, taking great care if a gouge is used not to split too much wood away, as the cut will be along the grain. Shape the exterior of the ears with a rat tail file finishing with strips of sandpaper. Form the central depression in the ear with a 1/4in (6mm) No.9, being very careful not to overweaken the ear. Draw on the forelock and define it with a 1/8in (3mm) No.10 removing the wood

from each side with a 1/4in (9mm) No.6 and forming the depression over the top of the eyebrow with the same tool. Make several random cuts down the forelock with a 1/8in (3mm) No.10 following the natural flow of the hair. Carve in the well-pronounced depression that runs from the back of the nostril to underneath the eyebrow with a 3/8in (9mm) No.6 (Fig 111).

The Eyes

The eye is formed in the same way as that used for previous animal carvings. The sphere of the eyeball is formed by stabbing down vertically with a suitably shaped gouge or by using the length of rod with a shallow sphere drilled in the end. The triangles of the front and rear of the eyeball are cut in either with a 1/8in (3mm) No.3 or a sharp pointed

158

craft knife. A shallow gouge cut with a 1/8in (3mm) No.10 is then made round the exterior of the eye and a small hole drilled in the eyeball centre with a large needle to form the shadow that brings the eye to life (Fig 111).

The Nostrils and Mouth

Mark in the nostrils, ensuring that there is sufficient space left to define the mouth clearly and that they are symmetrical, before carving in the central depression with a 1/8in (3mm) No.10. Remove wood from around the exterior of the nostril with a 3/8in (9mm) No.6 to give the flared effect and carefully round over the nostril top edge by filing with a small fine file. Define the mouth with a 1/8in (3mm) No.10.

The Mane

The mane on the carving illustrated was fairly evenly disposed on each side of the head, similar to the one on the horse's head described for a previous design. It may be felt that greater realism would be achieved if the mane was disposed more on one side of the neck than the other. If so, the drawing should be altered before the mane is carved.

Mark on the neck the main hanks of hair and the tendril that flows across the cheek and define them very deeply with a 3/8in (9mm) No.10 using a 1/8in (3mm) No.10 for the tendril (Fig 111). Mark on the shallow diagonal cuts that flow smoothly out of one channel into the next and define them with a 1/4in (6mm) No.9 (Fig 111). Finish the mane with a few random cuts following the natural flow of the hair on the remaining bare surfaces with a 1/8in (3mm) No.10.

Fig 112

The Flanks and Tail

All the big Shires are extremely muscular with great bunches of muscle over the chest, legs and flanks. These should be carved in very deeply with the edges well rounded over and contoured smoothly into the surrounding areas. Mark on all the muscles and define deeply with a 1/4in (6mm) No.9 removing the waste wood on the outside of the cut so formed with a 1/4in (6mm) No.3. Contour smoothly into the surrounding areas with riffler files and a small scraper ground up to the radius required. Note that the stifle is particularly prominent on the raised rear leg. Finish the tail, following the natural flow of the hair.

The Feathering

In some Shire horses the front tip of the hoof is visible beneath the feathering especially when the hair is tossed about by the action of the galloping horse. If you decide to show the tip of one or more hooves they should be defined

159

now and cleaned up before the carving of the feathering commences.

The hair of the feathering is carved in a similar manner and using the same gouges as were used for the tail and mane, but in this case, due to the action of the moving horse, the hair tends to swirl around the hoof. This movement can be clearly seen in Fig 113 on the front leg. The feathering on the inside of the hoof is difficult to get at (although it is not as difficult in this pose as it would be if the horse was stationary and the legs were together). A backbent 1/4in (6mm) No.10 and, if finances will stretch to it, a frontbent 1/4in (6mm) No.10 would be of great assistance here.

Both gouges are very useful additions to the tool kit when all the basic gouges have been acquired.

The Base

Texture the top surface of the base by making a series of clean, shallow gouge cuts across it with a 3/8in (9mm) No.6 and then rout a moulding or carve in a cove around the top edge with a 1/4in (6mm) No.9 if this was not done earlier when the top surface was roughly carved to allow for the hooves to be bosted in. Carve your mark on the base side and add the year (Fig 113).

Fig 113 The finished carving of the galloping Shire; country favourite.

Finishing

Scrape out all the remaining gouge marks and sand down all the easily sandable areas with reducing grades of sandpaper, using 0 grade steel wool to clean up the mane, tail and feathering carefully. Lightly dampen only the easily sandable areas to raise the grain and when thoroughly dry sand down the raised grain with well-worn sandpaper. I have already suggested that light-coloured sapwood could be used to indicate the white feathering. An alternative which often attracts my students is to carve the whole work in a light-coloured wood and then stain the required areas a darker colour. This practice is never satisfactory, though, and many hours of painstaking work can be ruined because once applied the stain cannot be satis-factorily removed. All the finishes described in the chapter on finishing would be suitable for this carving. The carving illustrated was varnished, rub-bed down and wax polished.

THE GREY WOLVES (SCALE 5)

Canis lupus

This proud and handsome carnivore has had a thoroughly undeserved reputation for centuries. It is in fact a peaceable animal, rarely, if ever, attacking man and living contentedly in packs of about fifteen animals. The rigid hierarchy of the pack is maintained by a ritualised behaviour that makes any real aggression unnecessary, except in times of real stress. The wolf is an opportunist, usu-ally taking only the sick and weaker animals of a herd and leaving the strong and healthy to breed and flourish. Its main prey are large mammals such as moose, caribou and elk, although in times of scarcity it will take hares, voles, lemmings and even beetles.

In the past the wolf's alert, intelligent shyness has made it a difficult animal for the hunter to kill, and in more recent years there has been a deeper and more sensitive understanding of its role in maintaining the delicate balance that exists between all creatures that inhabit the wilderness. Unlike many of the large mammals that have been, and still are being, hunted to extinction there is a cautious optimism for the continued sur-vival of this handsome and intelligent animal.

Although this is a more difficult carv-ing than those already described, the three elements of the design, the two wolves and the half-concealed caribou antler, are well separated and can be considered and dealt with as three sepa-rate problems. In fact, they could be carved quite separately if so desired, only the relevant sections of the text then being followed.

The ritualised, snarling aggression of one wolf and the quick alert stance of the other as it gazes out across the frozen tundra for possible danger are characteristic poses, and the base is indi-cative of the cruel frozen environment in which they are able to survive. The legs and paws are sunk into the soft snow and the shallow hollows left by the drifting snow are clearly visible behind the half-covered caribou antler (Figs 120 and 123).

To enable each animal to be readily identified in the text, the snarling wolf will be termed horizontal or Hor. wolf, and the upright wolf will be termed vertical or Vert. wolf.

Blocking in

The Bodies

As always the way in which the work is to be held while the carving proceeds should first be considered. A wood block screwed to the bottom of the base as in previous carvings will hold the work securely in the vice, but for this carving it needs to be about 3×3×4in (77×77×102mm) and screwed on very firmly indeed, the sandbag previously described will also be useful particularly in the early stages when a great deal of wood needs to be removed and some heavy bosting in blows are required.

For added realism both wolves are positioned at an angle to the base centre line. This means that the outline cannot be bandsawed out. A certain amount of waste wood could be removed with the bandsaw but the difficulty of determining exactly where the outline should be and the extra wood that needs to be left for safety makes this of limited use.

Mark on the top of the wood the outline shown in Fig 114 and remove wood from outside the lines with a 5/8in (15mm) No.7 and carver's mallet, clean-ing up the ragged surface left with a surform and ensuring that the sides are vertical. Some help can be obtained in removing the waste wood by making a series of sawcuts across the accessible surfaces and then splitting the wood along the grain.

Produce three templates from the side-view drawing, one showing the complete side view, and a template of each of the individual wolves. Position the individual templates on the side of the wood, adjusting their position by reference to the complete template and repeat on the other side of the wood, taking great care to see that they are lined up by reference to lines drawn across the top of the block using a set square. Once the block has been marked out, remove wood from outside the lines with a 5/8in (15mm) No.7 leaving blocks of wood sufficient to carve the heads in the head positions of both wolves, and a sufficiently large block for the caribou antler. Leave only a small gap between the antler and the Hor. wolf's front paw, sufficiently only for the front leg to be defined. Remove wood seen between the legs from the side, removing the bulk of the waste by drilling through and then removing the rest of the waste wood with a 3/8in (9mm) No.10 and a 3/8in (9mm) No.6. Remove the unwanted

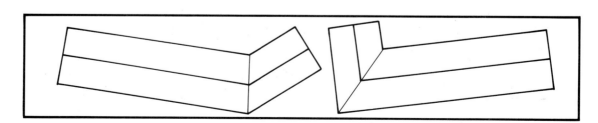

Fig 114 Marking out the top view of the block.

Fig 115 Template for the left-hand (vertical) wolf on the group carving of two grey wolves.

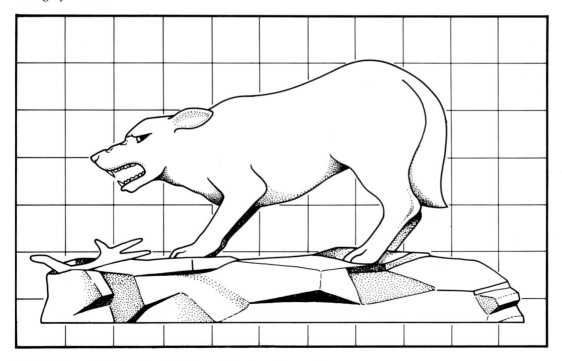

Fig 116 Template for the right-hand (horizontal) wolf.

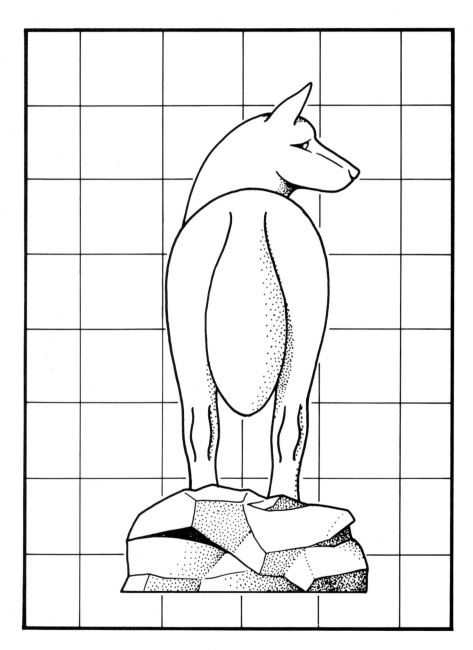

Fig 117 Template for the left-hand wolf – back view.

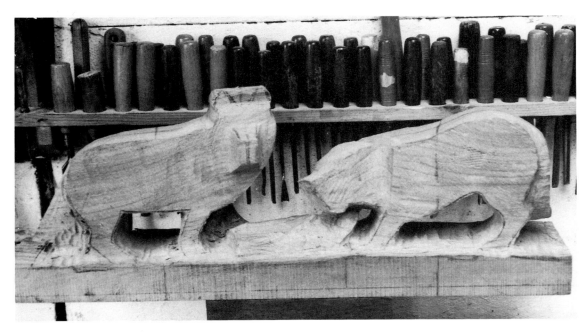

Fig 118

legs down to about halfway into the block. It will all tend to look very ragged now, and confidence will be lost unless it is all cleaned up as far as is reasonably possible with a round surform (Fig 118). Remove wood from each side of the tails, which are thick and bushy, and at the same time define the backs of the rear legs (Fig 119).

Draw on the back and front views, noting that all legs are closer together at the bottom than the top, with the exception of those of the Hor. wolf whose front paws are straddled wide apart. Remove wood from outside the lines with a 5/8in (15mm) No.7.

The Heads

Simply turning a head adds very considerably to the interest and realism of a bird or animal carving, but it also adds to the difficulty of blocking it in. As a general rule the body is first blocked in

Fig 119

165

leaving a square block in the head position as we have already done with the
wolves. A centre line is then drawn on
the top of the head block at the required
angle from the body centre line, and if
the head is to be upright, as in the
Vert. wolf, a centre line is drawn vertically down the front of the head block.
Two parallel lines are then drawn on
the top of the head block a head width
apart, each side of the centre line, and
also down the front of the block. In the
case of the Hor. wolf the head is not
only slightly turned but also angled over
(see Fig 120). In this case the lines on
the front of the head block will not be
vertical but drawn in at the required
angle. Now remove wood from outside
the two parallel lines with a 5/8in (15mm)
No.7. Produce a template of each head
and use them to mark out the head
shapes on each side of the two blocks,
carefully ensuring that they are symmetrical. Remove wood from outside the
lines using a rat tail file for the final
shaping and cleaning up.

The two heads should be blocked in
and turned at the required angle by
now, and in the case of the Hor. wolf
angled over as well. I have detailed this
method of turning a head at some length
because it is often a problem that confronts the carver, and it may well be
found to be of use in subsequent and
perhaps more complex works, where
the body is turned and twisted as well
as the head.

Bosting In

The Bodies

Because both heads are turned, the head
and neck cannot be contoured smoothly
and naturally into the body until the
body has been bosted in and its shape
established. Bost in both bodies, frequently consulting photographs and
drawings of wolves throughout. It is at
this important stage of the work that
the carving comes to life, the snarling
menace of the one wolf and the alert
awareness of the other start to become
evident. It will be found that only by
detailed research and a deep understanding of the wolf will an exciting and
interesting work be achieved. This is
true of course of all carving of natural
forms.

The Heads

First define the ears of the Hor. wolf
with a 3/16in (4.5mm) No.10 removing
the surrounding waste wood with a
3/8in (9mm) No.6. Then remove the
wood from between the ears of the Vert.
wolf with a fretsaw after first ensuring
that the external shape is absolutely
correct. Use a medium-cut rat tail file
for the final shaping and cleaning up
of both ears. Note that there is a marked
depression in the centre of the skulls,
starting between the eyebrows and tapering off just before the ears are reached
(Fig 122), and that the necks, because
of the wrinkled coat, are very wide.

Carving the Head Details

The eyes are well defined, intelligent
and piercing. Form the spherical eyeball
as described for previous animal carvings
ensuring that in this case they are
strongly defined. Cut in deeply the
triangles of the front and back corners
of the eyeball with a 1/8in (3mm) No.3
or a sharp pointed craft knife and then

166

Fig 120

carve in a shallow depression round the exterior of the eye with a 1/8in (3mm) No.10. Form a small but deep hole in the centre of the eyeball with the point of a large needle to give the black shadow that will bring the eye to life and give the piercing look. Take great care not to split the eyeball when twisting in the needle.

The nostrils are cut in with a 1/16in (1.5mm) No.10 or by two inclined cuts made with a sharp craft knife. Note that the cuts widen out towards the centre of the nostrils (Fig 122).

The Mouths

The mouth of the Vert. Wolf is quite simply cut in with the 1/16in (1.5mm) No.10. The mouth of the Hor. wolf, however, is much more difficult. First define the shape of the open mouth with a 1/8in (3mm) No.10, lowering the wood between the gouge marks with a 1/8in

(3mm) No.3. Mark in the long tearing canine teeth and the molars and remove wood from between the upper and lower sets of teeth by first drilling away as much of the waste wood as possible with a small twist drill, and then removing the rest with a 1/8in (3mm) No.10 and a 1/8in (3mm) No.3, cleaning up the mouth afterwards with suitably shaped fine files. When drilling in, enter the drill from both sides of the mouth to ensure that it does not wander too far off-centre. The long canine teeth should be roughly shaped with a suitably shaped fine file, followed by sanding with strips of fine sandpaper. The sandpaper can also be used for the final shaping of the canines.

To define the molars realistically it is sufficient only to make small V cuts between each tooth with a small V tool or a sharp craft knife (Fig 121).

Fig 121

The Muscles, Bone Structure and Fur

Unlike other powerful smooth-coated mammals, the muscle and bone structure is not clearly visible. It can, however, still just be seen, particularly on the legs and flanks. Mark in all the muscles and define them with a 3/8in (9mm) No.6 by making very shallow cuts and then rounding over the edges of the cuts and contouring them smoothly into the legs and flanks with a rat tail file. Because of its density and thickness the fur tends to wrinkle up round the neck when the head is turned and also across the shoulders and flanks. This wrinkling

Fig 122

can be clearly seen in Figs 121 and 122. Carve in the shallow wrinkles on the body with a 3/8in (9mm) No.6, using a 1/4in (6mm) No.10 for the deeper and more clearly defined wrinkles round the neck.

The Paws

Only two paws are visible above the snow. They should first be formed into a ball with a 1/4in (6mm) No.3 and then cleaned up with strips of fine sandpaper. Form a shallow depression round the front of each paw and about halfway up with a rat tail file and then cut in the three depressions between the toes with a 1/8in (3mm) No.10 (Figs 122 and 124).

Texturing the Fur

Texturing the coat of an animal carving to indicate fur will sometimes look unreal or even detract from an attractive grain. It should only be done after much careful thought and by experimenting on a spare piece of wood. In the case of the wolves, however there is little doubt that the texturing adds very considerably to the realism and is very well worth the time and effort involved. The coats are textured with a 1/8in (3mm) No.10 by making a series of approximately 1/2in (12mm) long cuts at close intervals following the natural flow of the hair. The gouge should be allowed to run out of the wood at the end of each cut to produce a point.

Fig 123

The Antler

The caribou antler is partially buried by the driving snow which is both realistic and provides solid support for what would otherwise be a thin vulnerable section. Slope the top surface of the block (which was previously left to carve in the antler) to the required angle with a 3/8in (9mm) No.6. Clean up the surface with a scraper to enable the accurate shape of the antler to be drawn on. Define the antler with a 1/4in (6mm) No.9, removing the waste wood surrounding it with a 3/8in (9mm) No.6. Take care not to remove too much wood but leave the antler partially buried. Round over the edges of the antler with a 1/4in (6mm) No.3 and clean them up with a small fine flat file and fine sandpaper. Cut in the channels in the snow that have been formed by the wind, noting how they taper off. Texture the antler with a 1/8in (3mm) No.10.

The Base

The base is snow covered with only the blurred outlines of rocks showing through. Mark on all the rocks in ways that naturally suggest themselves to you and define them very deeply with a 3/8in (9mm) No.10, repeating several times if necessary in order to get down to the required depth. Take advantage of the gaps between the wolves' legs to recess the base deeply to get the full dramatic effect. Gently round over the rock edges to indicate both weathering and where the snow has partially covered them using a rat tail file.

This carving is a fairly difficult and

Fig. 124   The fairly complicated carving of a pair of grey wolves finished.

complex one, and if it has been success-fully completed in an interesting and lively way it will almost certainly be cared for and perhaps last for very many years giving pleasure and satisfaction to many people. They will want to know who the artist craftsman was, so use a suitably flat rock surface to carve on your mark and the year.

Finishing

This is a particularly difficult carving to clean up as it is only possible to sand the smooth areas of the base. The rest of the work can be lightly rubbed down with 0 grade steel wool. A fine grade flap-wheel fitted to an electric drill and used with great restraint would clean it up without sanding over crisply-carved edges. Any of the finishes described in the chapter on finishing would be suit-able for this work but the easiest to apply and probably the most attractive would be two or three coats of Rustin's Danish oil, lightly buffed up when thoroughly dry with a lint-free cloth.

THE UNICORN (SCALE 5)

Part 1

I have been given to understand, on the impeccable authority of the six-year-old daughter of a friend, that because of its gentle good nature the unicorn, if insulted, will lie down and die. It was with the greatest trepidation, therefore, that I undertook this commission but by the exercise of a considerable amount of restraint the work was successfully com-pleted, and I am pleased to be able to

to be able to report that the unicorn has settled down and appears to be completely happy in its new home.

All the techniques and methods used to carve the works in the preceding pages are used for the unicorn, but with the addition of inlay. The successful completion of this work will bring the carver up to a standard that will enable him to undertake most forms of carving in the future with confidence.

Work on the inlay is only begun when all the other work is complete, right up to the end of the rubbing down stage, so the carving and inlay can be regarded as two entirely separate problems. The inlay can be disregarded until the carving is finished, in fact, it can be omitted altogether if so desired.

This pose makes full use of the elegant beauty of this mythical beast but the slender legs are vulnerable to damage. This was partly overcome by carving the legs a little thicker than would nor-mally be expected and by arranging the grain to run vertically up the legs. Also the tail forms part of the extended right rear leg and is firmly attached to the base for strength. The resulting rather ornate base was intended not only to support the carving but also to balance and complement it.

The wood used for the work illustrated was Cornish elm, *Ulmus stricta*, the white of the inlay showing up particu-larly well against its chocolate brown colour. Any dark hardwood would be suitable and even a light-coloured oak or chestnut could be used if it was fumed later to a darker colour. In this case, though, the inlay would first need to be tested in ammonia fumes to ensure that it was not discoloured by them.

This work was inlaid with bone, the

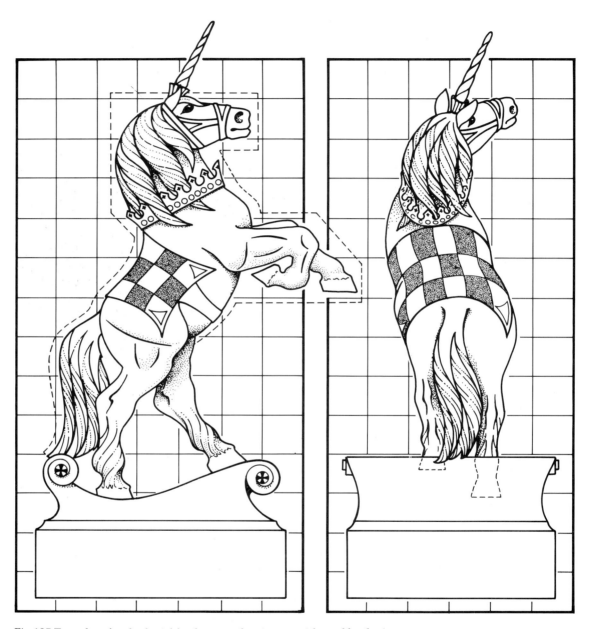

Fig 125 Template for the lavishly-decorated unicorn – side and back views.

preparation of which can be found in Chapter 8. A white hardwood would provide just as effective a contrast and is much easier to work than the bone, but on no account should an attempt be made to use a soft white wood which, because of its different density, sands away more quickly than the surrounding hardwood, forming unsightly hollows. The description of the inlaying in the text will assume that wood is used for the inlay and not bone.

Because all the animal carvings previously described were designed to stand four square the question of balance has not yet been considered. The unicorn, however, with its large heavy head turned to the right, must inevitably move its body to the left in order to counterbalance the weight. You can demonstrate this by standing at ease; your chin will then be central above your two feet. If your weight is moved on to one foot your chin will automatically move over until it is directly above the load-bearing foot. The effect of this can be seen in Fig 126. It is of the greatest importance that this effect is taken into account whenever out of balance forces are part of a design.

Unicorns are sometimes pictured with a beard. If it is felt that a beard would be desirable the drawing should be altered now before the carving is blocked in.

To balance the weight of the turned head the body of the unicorn not only leans to the left but is also turned at a slight angle to the base centre line. This turning of the body makes it impossible to bandsaw out an accurate outline. A template of the side view should therefore be produced, following the dotted line on the drawing which allows for

Fig 126

the extra wood required. A block of wood should be left in the head position to allow the head to be turned. Use the template to mark out the side view on the block of wood and remove wood from outside the lines, either with a bandsaw or by sawing in radially at close intervals, then splitting the wood away along the grain with a 5/8in (15mm) No. 7 and a carver's mallet. Clean up the ragged outlines with a round surform.

Screw the 3×3×4in (77×77×102mm) wood block, used to hold the previous carvings, firmly to the bottom of the base. This will hold the work securely in the vice. Because of the height of

Fig 127

Fig 128

the carving and the need to remove a lot of wood from the head position, an 18in (458mm) square sandbag should be used to hold the work while the heavy bosting in is being carried out. This will prevent any possible damage to the slender and vulnerable legs.

Blocking In

Mark on the back of the body the curved centre line and draw a parallel line on each side of it a body width apart (Fig 126). Remove wood from outside the lines with a 5/8in (15mm) No. 7 and at the same time angle the body block to the left. Do not remove wood, however, from either the head block or the front right leg which is angled outwards and

requires the full width of the block. The side view can now be drawn accurately on the side of the body block and wood removed from outside the lines with the 5/8in (15mm) No. 7, cleaning the surface up with a round surform. Draw on the rear view of the tail (Fig 126) and remove wood from each side of it. At the same time define the shape of the back of the right rear leg leaving an excess of wood where the tail joins the leg to be removed later, when the inside shape of the leg has been accurately determined.

Turning the Head

Draw a centre line on the top of the head block at the required angle from

Fig 129

Fig 130

the body centre line and also down the front of the block. This front centre line is at an angle as the head is not only turned but also angled over, as all heads are when they are turned. Try turning your own head and you will see what I mean. Draw a parallel line each side of the centre lines, a head width apart, and remove wood from outside the lines with a 5/8in (15mm) No. 7. Clean up with a round surform. Produce a template of the head and use it to mark out each side of the head block, taking great care to ensure that it is symmetrical. Remove wood from outside the lines and clean up the head with a rat tail file; the head should by now be blocked in, turned and angled over.

At this point the head may not appear to marry up with the body. The bosting in will correct this.

Draw on the shape of the front legs, noting that the right leg is angled out to the right (Fig 127). Remove wood from between both them and the rear legs once the external shape has been accurately established.

Bosting In

Because the head harness, crown, and saddle cloth take the same shape as the head, neck and body of the unicorn they can be safely ignored during the bosting in, except to leave a small extra thickness of wood for the harness and rather more on the neck in the crown position.

175

The single horn has a marked effect on the appearance of the whole unicorn and particularly the head. It would be advisable, therefore, to produce a horn now as described in Part 2 so that it can be viewed and taken into account whilst the bosting in takes place, even if it is only held temporarily in place by hand.

Bost in the whole unicorn removing the bulk of the waste with a 5/8in (15mm) No. 7 and then using a round surform for the final shaping and cleaning up (Fig 128).

Clean up the surface of the whole carving with a scraper in order that the harness, mane, and crown can be clearly and accurately drawn on as shown in Fig 129.

The Head

Shape the exterior of the ears with a rat tail file, ensuring that the shape is correct before removing wood from between them with a fretsaw. Define all the head harness with a 1/8in (3mm) No. 10 and lower the wood between the straps with a 1/4in (6mm) No. 3 to a depth of about 1/8in (3mm). Draw on the forelock and define it with a 1/8in (3mm) No. 10 and then make a few random cuts down it with the same tool, following the natural flow of the hair.

The Eye

The eye is formed using the same tools and methods as for the previous animal carvings. The sphere of the eyeball is first formed, then triangles are cut in at the front and rear of the eyeball and a small channel gouged round the exterior of the eye. A small hole is also pierced in the centre of the eyeball to bring it to life.

The Nostrils, Mouth and Beard

Mark in the nostrils, noting that they are situated right on the end of the muzzle, and define the central depression with a 1/8in (3mm) No. 10 taking great care not to crumble the edges of the nostrils. It would be safer to make several shallow cuts than attempt to cut them in one cut. Remove wood from around the outer edge of the nostril with a 3/16in (4.5mm) No. 6 to give the flared effect (Fig 130).

The mouth is simply cut in with a 1/8in (3mm) No. 10. the edges are rounded over with a small fine flat file.

If it has been decided to include a beard it should be shaped now and the surface textured by long cuts with a 1/8in (3mm) No. 10 following the natural, curving flow of the hair.

The small radius left by the 1/8in (3mm) No. 10 when it was used to define the head harness should now be removed and the angle sharpened up with a sharp pointed craft knife. This will define the harness more clearly.

The Crown and Mane

Deeply define the large hanks of hair of the mane already drawn on the neck and shown in Fig 129 with a 3/8in (9mm) No. 10 using a 1/8in (3mm) No. 10 to make a more shallow cut where they cross the crown, define the top and bottom edges of the crown with a 3/16 (4.5mm) No. 10 avoiding the hanks of hair that cross it. Remove wood from

Fig 131

Fig 132

the crown on each side of the hanks of hair to indicate that they are flowing across it (Fig 130). Draw on the shallow diagonal cuts that flow smoothly from one side of the main hanks of hair to the other with a 1/4in (6mm) No. 9 and then make a series of small random cuts on any of the bare surfaces left with a 1/8in (3mm) No. 10, following the natural flow of the hair (Figs 131 and 132).

The surface of the crown is concave. Carve in the depression with a 3/8in (9mm) No. 6 using a small, fine half-round file for the final shaping and cleaning up (Fig 130).

Mark on the gaps between the spikes at the top of the crown and drill a shallow hole in each one with a suitably sized drill. The spikes can then be pointed by stabbing down vertically with a 1/4in (6mm) No. 3. The waste chip is removed with a 1/8in (3mm) No. 3 (Figs 131 and 132).

The Body Harness

Define all the body harness and saddle cloth with a 1/8in (3mm) No. 10, removing the waste wood on the body to a depth of about 1/8in (3mm) with a 3/8in (9mm) No. 6. Sharpen up the radius left by the 1/8in (3mm) No. 10 with a sharp pointed craft knife to make the harness stand out clearly. Clean up the gouge marks on the body with a riffler file followed by a scraper (Fig 130).

177

Fig 133 The detail here shows the challenge offered by the intricacy of the design.

The Legs and Hooves

Draw all the muscles on the flanks and legs and define them with a 3/16in (4.5mm) No. 10 removing the waste wood with a 1/4in (6mm) No. 3 and using a riffler file and small scraper to contour them smoothly into the legs and flanks. Carve on the curving feathering on the rear of the rear legs with a 1/8in (3mm) No. 10.

The hooves are cloven. Form the V at the front of the hoof with a 3/8in (9mm) 60° V tool or by making two inclined cuts with a sharp craft knife. The small depression behind the hoof is formed by stabbing down vertically with a 1/4in (6mm) No. 9 and then removing the waste chip with a 1/8in (3mm) No. 3 (Figs 131 and 137).

The Tail

The hair of the tail is carved in a similar manner to the mane. Draw on the tail the main curving hanks of hair that flow from the top to the bottom and define them very deeply with a 3/8in (9mm) No. 10 repeating several times in order to get down to the required depth. Draw on the shallow cuts that run diagonally across the main hanks of hair and define them with a 1/4in (6mm) No. 9. Make a series of random cuts carefully with a 1/8in (3mm) No. 10 for the natural flow of the hair on the remaining bare areas of the tail (Figs 133 and 136).

The Base

Plane or sand up the sides of the base before routing in the cove. Define the curlicues on the top four corners of the base by stabbing down vertically with a gouge whose sweep fits the shape of the curlicues. Remove the waste wood surrounding them with the edge of a 5/8in (15mm) No. 7, using the same tool to form the concave shape between the cove and the curlicues.

Carve in the curlicue spiral with a 1/8in (3mm) No. 10 leaving a 3/16in (4.5mm) circle in the centre to be drilled later to take the spigot of the rosette (Figs 134, 136 and 137). Sand up the whole base, taking great care to achieve a very high standard of finish and then

Fig 134

Fig 135

carve on your mark and the year of carving.

Decorating the Harness

The head harness was decorated with a small rosette-shaped punch which was used to form a series of small rosettes at close intervals along the straps leaving sufficient space for the inlay. The same punch was used to decorate the tail strap at the rear of the saddle cloth (Figs 133 and 136). This rosette punch is readily available at specialist carvers' suppliers.

The centre of the saddle cloth is con-

cave. Form the depression with a rat tail and fine half-round file using strips of reducing grades of sandpaper for the final shaping and finishing. Stick masking or sticky tape to the back of the sandpaper to prevent it breaking. Ensure that there is a high standard of finish on the surface of the saddle cloth before applying the decoration. Mark out the decorative pattern on the saddle cloth, leaving sufficient room for the inlay, and then define the edges of the squares with a 1/8in (3mm) No. 10. Texture the surface of every other square with a nail which has had its point rounded by filing or grinding. Tap it at close intervals into the surface of the wood (Figs 133 and 136).

Cut small diamond shapes in the bottom of the spikes of the crown with a sharp pointed craft knife (Fig 132).

Part 2

The Inlay

If marrow bone is to be used for the inlay it should first be prepared following the instructions in Chapter 8.

There is a wide choice of native white hardwoods that are readily available in the small quantities required for inlay. Holly is about the most suitable as it is very white and dense and contrasts well with darker woods. Lime and box are also ideal inlay woods, the light cream of lime and the creamy yellow of box sometimes harmonising better with the colour of the base wood than the much whiter holly. The choice of a suitable inlay wood is very much dependent upon the colour and warmth of the base wood, and this should be taken into account when making a choice.

When inlay is contemplated it is often possible to find a small misshapen bough that can be removed from a suitable tree without damaging the tree or upsetting its appearance. The bark should be removed and the bough sawn into strips approximately 1/2in (12mm) thick. The strips should be stored in an airy, sunless place with spacers between them to allow the air to flow through. A small weight on top will help to resist curling.

The Unicorn's Horn

Saw out a length of 1/2in (12mm) square inlay wood by 3in (76mm) long and file off the edges to form a rough dowel. Use a hand brace to drive the dowel down through a 1/2in (12mm) hole in a dowel plate so producing a clean, accurate 1/2×3 1/2 (12×89mm) dowel. Reduce one end of the dowel to 1/4in (6mm) diameter roughly with a file and then drive it down through 1/4in (6mm) hole in the dowel plate to form an accurate spigot that will fit into a hole drilled between the unicorn's ears. The spigot should be about 1/4in (6mm) long. Reduce the diameter of the rest of the dowel to 1/4in (6mm) with a file leaving a short length about 3/8in (9mm) long next to the spigot on which to carve the crown. This is situated at the bottom of the horn and can just be seen in Figs 131 and 135. Taper the horn off towards the tip with files and then clean it up. Complete the tapering smoothly by holding the spigot in the chuck of an electric drill, sanding the horn with strips of sandpaper whilst the horn rotates.

Taper the small crown towards its base with a file and again clean it up in an electric drill. Make a series of small V cuts about 1/8in (3mm) apart down the crown to form the small divisions round it. Mark in the spiral on the horn and file it in with a rat tail file of a suitable diameter, reducing the size of the spiral towards the tip. Check the angle of the horn between the unicorn's ears ensuring that it is satisfactory before drilling in a 1/4in (6mm) hole to accept the spigot of the horn. It is advisable not to glue the horn in place as it is fairly vulnerable to damage and it may have to be removed later for packing or repair.

The Rosettes

The decorative rosettes inserted in the crown are made up by first producing a length of 1/8in (3mm) dowel in the dowel plate and then drilling a series of 1/8in (3mm) holes in the crown about 3/16in (4.5mm) deep. Bevel the end of the dowel slightly with a file so that it will enter the 1/8in (3mm) hole freely without crushing the rim. Tap it gently into the hole after first applying a dab of adhesive. Saw off the protruding end of the dowel with a junior hacksaw blade leaving approximately 1/8in (3mm) protruding. Round over the head of the protruding dowel with a file or alternatively drill a shallow hole in the end of a short length of rod of a suitable diameter and make a saw cut across it to clear the waste wood. This will produce an accurate and clean dome quickly when it is placed over the end of the dowel and rotated slowly in a handbrace. File two small V-shaped cuts at right angles to each other on the top of the dome to form the rosette.

The larger rosettes situated in the centre of the curlicues on the four corners of the base are formed in the same way as the crown rosettes except that a 3/16in (4.5mm) spigot is first formed on the end of the 1/2in (12mm) dowel in the same way that the horn spigot was formed. This ensures that there is no slight gap visible when the rosette is tapped home and that it is only necessary to drill a 3/16in (4.5mm) hole in the curlicue centre for the spigot.

Inserting the Inlay

The use of inlay in this carving was very restrained in order not to overpower the other decorative effects such as the punch marks and texturing. It may be considered that some extra inlay would be more effective. This could easily be done if required by using the following method.

Produce a template of the required inlay shape, preferably on a paper of a colour which will show up well against the inlay wood, and hold it in the inlay position to check for accuracy. Glue the template to a piece of 3/16 (5mm) thick inlay wood with contact adhesive so that it will be held firmly and yet can be easily removed before the adhesive has had time to set. Ensure that there is sufficient inlay wood to enable it to be held whilst it is being fretsawed out. Fretsaw out the inlay and clean up any ragged edges that there may be with a fine file. Most of the inlay on the carving is inserted into convex surfaces so file the back of the inlay with a half-round file to make it a reasonable fit on the surface into which it is to be inserted. Remove the template from the inlay wood and glue the inlay into position using a contact adhesive.

When the inlay is reasonably firmly held, carefully mark round the edge with the point of a sharp craft knife, angling the knife outwards slightly to ensure that its tip accurately follows the inlay outline. Remove the inlay before the glue has had time to harden and then deepen the knife cut slightly with the tip of the craft knife. It is important here not to force the knife into the wood otherwise an ugly gap will be formed between the inlay and its recess. Remove the wood from the recess between the knife marks with a 1/8in (3mm) No. 3 and then repeat the process until the recess is about 1/8in (3mm) deep.

Fig 136

Fig 137

It is not necessary for the underside of the inlay to match the bottom of the recess exactly, as a gap-filling epoxy resin adhesive is used which will fill any slight irregularities. In fact, a slight roughness on both faces will assist the adherence of the glue. Check the fit of the inlay and adjust if necessary with a fine file, then tap it gently into position after first coating the back with an epoxy resin adhesive that is suitable for use with wood. When the adhesive is thoroughly dry the inlay should be filed flush with the surrounding wood. Any attempt to sand the inlay flat will usually result in either a depression or it standing slightly proud due to the difference in the hardness of the two woods. Damping the inlay will cause it to swell, making it a tighter fit in its recess.

Finishing

Great care should be taken when finishing this carving to ensure that the inlay wood is not discoloured by the finish used. In some woods, particularly the lighter-coloured woods used for inlay, oils will almost certainly discolour them and reduce the contrast between the inlay and the base wood. A test piece should always be experimented with before any type of finish is decided upon.

Probably the safest finish of all is the one used for the majority of the carvings in this book and the one illustrated – varnishing, rubbing down and then wax polishing. In this case care was taken not to remove too much varnish from the inlay wood so leaving it protected from any possible discolouration by the wax.

If a light-coloured oak or chestnut has been used with the intention of fuming it to a darker colour the inlay wood should already have been checked to ensure that it is impervious to ammonia fumes. The carving should be placed in a box, preferably with a glass or plastic front, so that the change in colour can be checked without exposure to the rather unpleasant ammonia fumes. It is then surrounded with wide-topped receptacles such as saucers into which the ammonia is poured, ensuring that no part of the carving is exposed to more of the fumes than another, otherwise a dark patch will result. The darkening process can be stopped at any time by simply removing the carving from exposure to the fumes. It can then be varnished, rubbed down and wax polished.

Glossary

Acanthus leaf Shape widely used for decorative carving.

Arkansa A natural sharpening stone.

Bass wood American white wood or lime.

Bosting in Roughing out the design on the block of wood.

Burl Growth on a tree caused by the gall beetle, containing wild and attractive growth patterns.

Cartouche Centre piece in the form of a roll of parchment.

Carver's bench screw Tapered screw for holding heavy carvings.

Cavetto Moulding shape.

Chamfer Moulding shape.

Check A fault in wood, such as a crack.

Chip carving Triangular-shaped chips cut in with a chip carving knife, usually in geometric patterns.

Classical Moulding shape.

Cove Moulding shape.

Diaper Repeat pattern.

Dowel Short round length of wood used for jointing and inlay.

Fitch Thin sheet of wood used for inlay or veneer.

Fluter Small U-shaped gouge.

Fuming Method of darkening certain wood types by exposing them to ammonia fumes.

Gesso Mixture used to coat wood before gilding; can be carved.

Ground Recessing a background.

Grounding tool Frontbent, flattish gouge used to recess backgrounds.

Linden Original name of lime wood.

Ogee Moulding shape.

Ovolo Moulding shape.

Parting tool A V tool.

Quick gouge Small U-shaped gouge.

Riffler Small elongated S-shaped file.

Roman ogee Moulding shape.

Rounding over Moulding shape.

Scratch stock Used to shape small mouldings.

Serif Triangular cuts formed at the end of letters.

Setting in Defining a design with a quick gouge.

Sinking Recessing the background of a relief.

Slipstone Sharpening stones with radii on two edges used to remove the wire edge on the inside of gouges.

Sweep The curve of a gouge.

Sapwood Light-coloured wood between the bark and the darker heartwood.

Shake Similar to a check.

Thundershake Fault in wood caused by extreme whipping of the sapling during violent storms.

Undercut To cut in the edge of a design at an inwards angle.

Veiner Small quick gouge.

Washita Natural sharpening stone.

Index

Other crafts titles available from The Crowood Press:

0 946284 54 7	*The Complete Guide to Metalworking*	Mike George
1 85223 717 1	*Pottery – A Manual of Techniques*	Doug Wensley
1 85223 175 0	*Bookbinding – A Manual of Techniques*	Pamela Richmond
1 85223 723 6	*Woodturning – A Manual of Techniques*	Hugh O'Neill
1 85223 195 5	*Furniture Making – A Manual of Techniques*	Anthony Hontoir
1 85223 195 5	*Jewellery Making – A Manual of Techniques*	David Rider
1 85223 427 X	*Relief Printmaking – A Manual of Techniques*	Colin Walklin
1 85223 196 3	*Torchon Lacemaking – A Manual of Techniques*	Elizabeth Wade
1 85223 583 7	*Woodcarving – Step-by-Step Techniques*	Jeremy Williams
1 85223 582 9	*Wood Finishing – Step-by-Step Techniques*	Den Hatchard
1 85223 758 9	*Wood Joints – Step-by-Step Techniques*	Anthony Hontoir
1 85223 759 7	*Woodturning – Step-by-Step Techniques*	Oliver Plant
1 85223 501 2	*The Craft of Stickmaking – Projects*	Leo Gowan
1 85223 454 7	*Rocking Horses – Projects*	Margaret Spencer
1 85223 449 0	*Wooden Toys – Projects*	Anthony Hontoir
1 85223 740 6	*Pine Furniture Making*	Anthony Hontoir